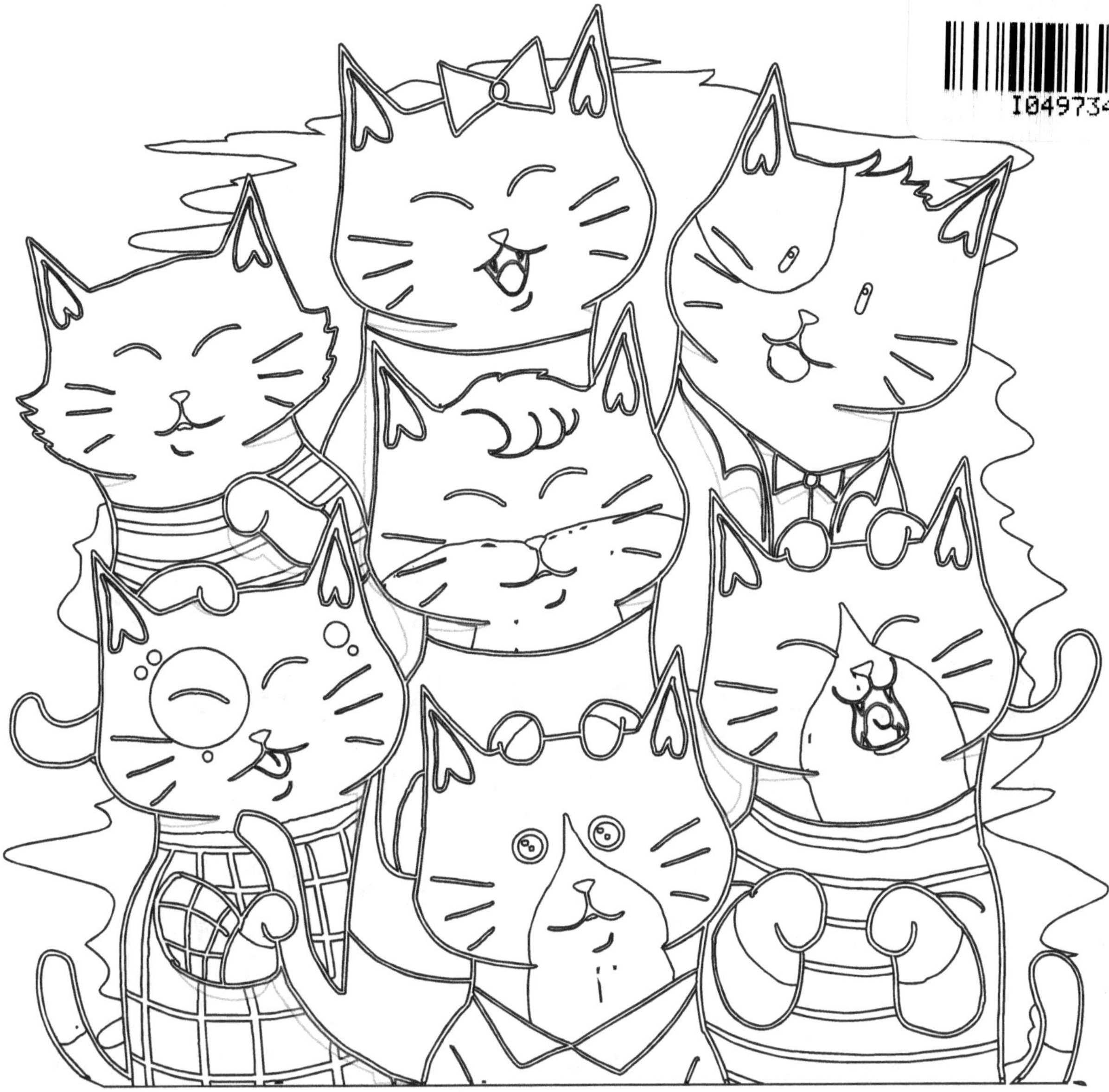

This coloring book belongs to:

Artwork by
www.Vecteezy.com

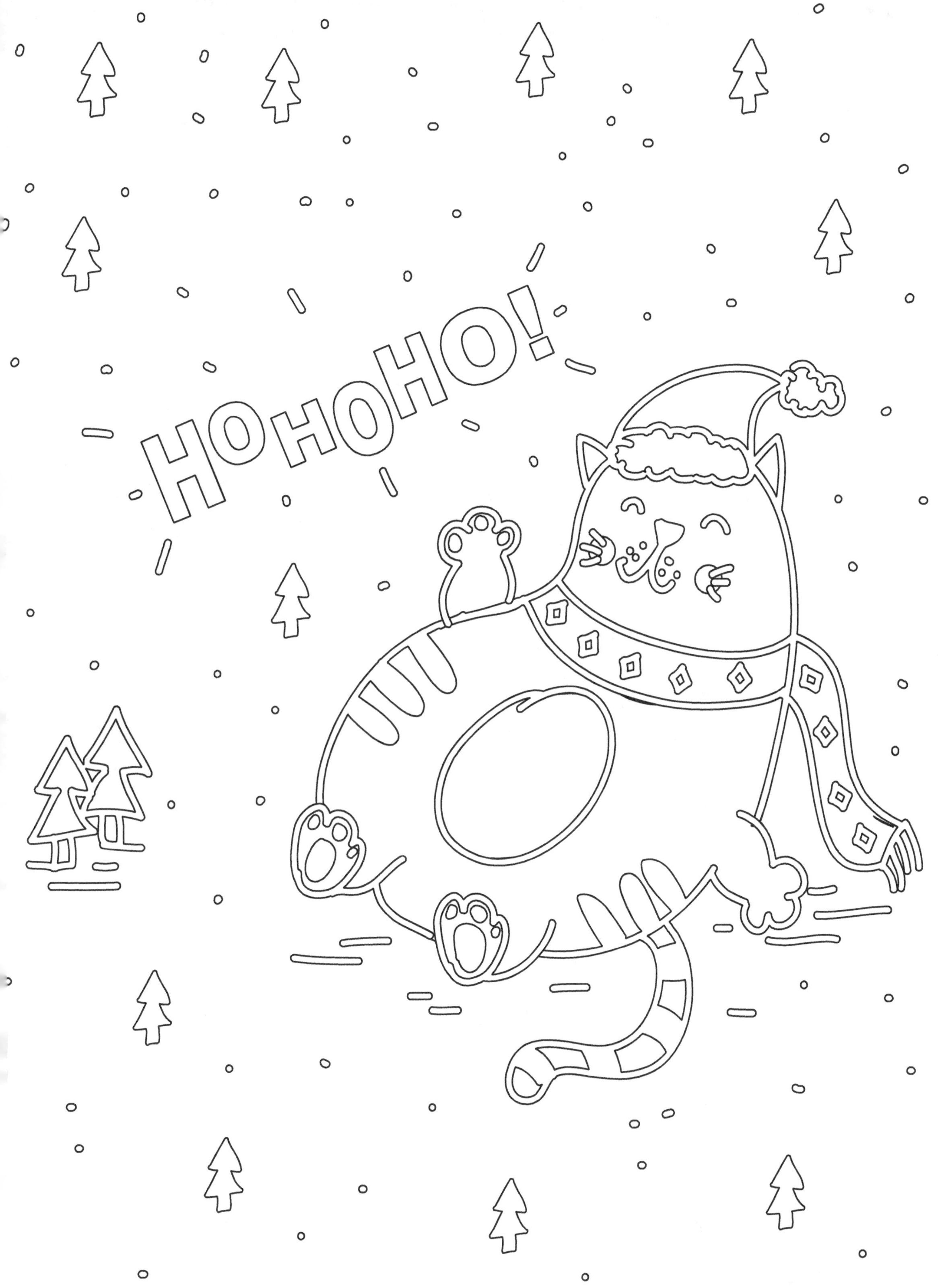
HOHOHO!

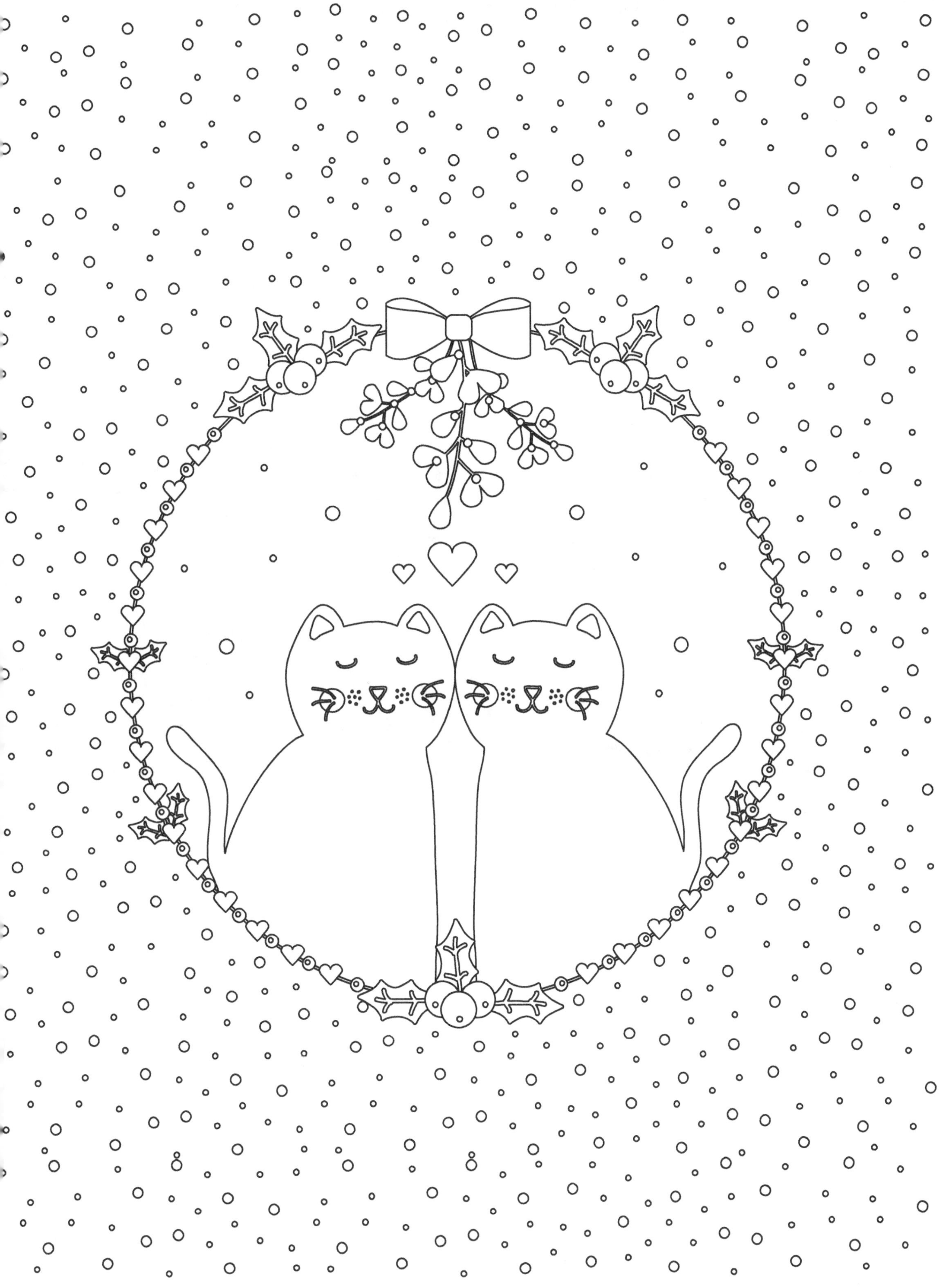

KEEP
CALM
and
Merry
Christmas

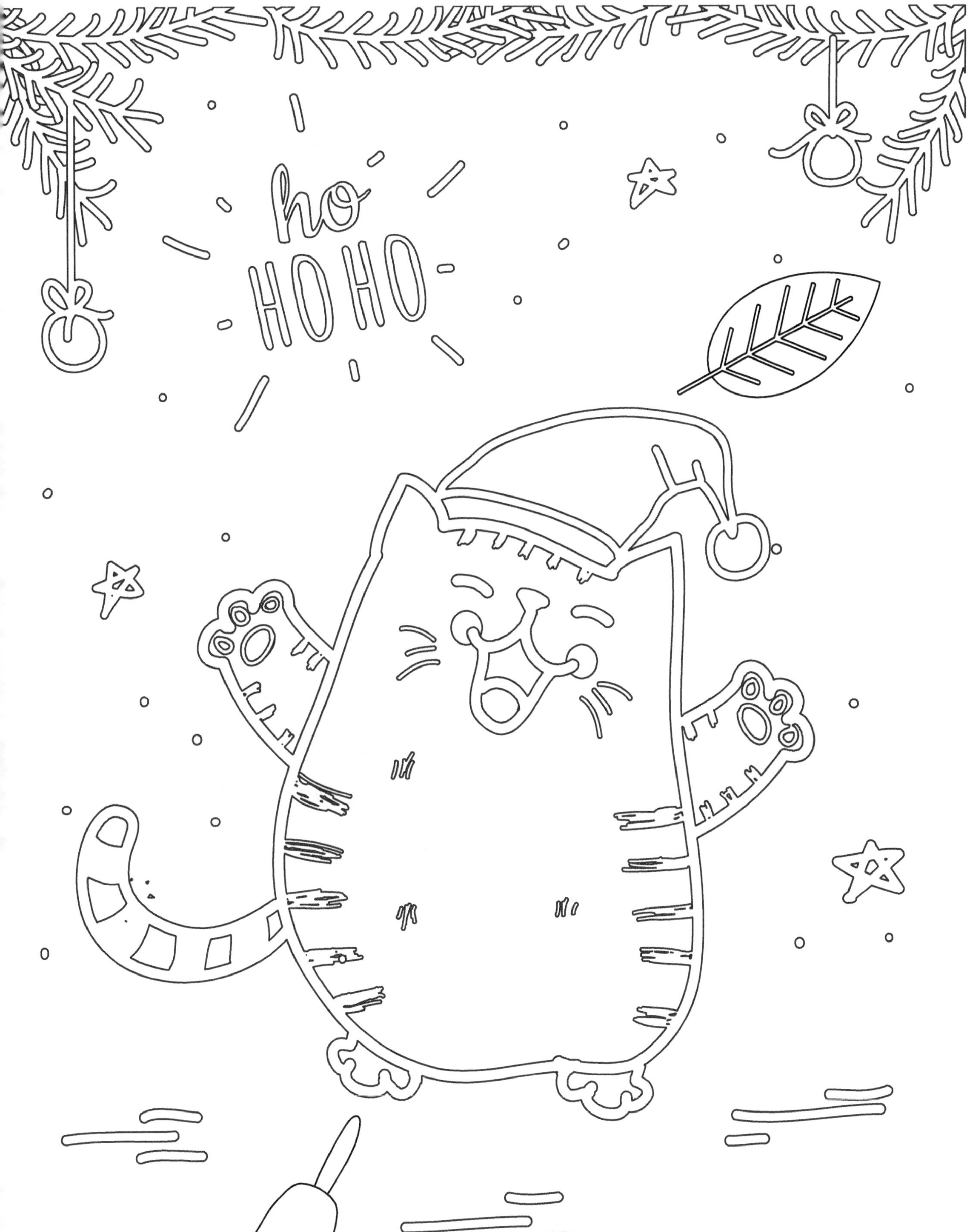
ho
HO HO

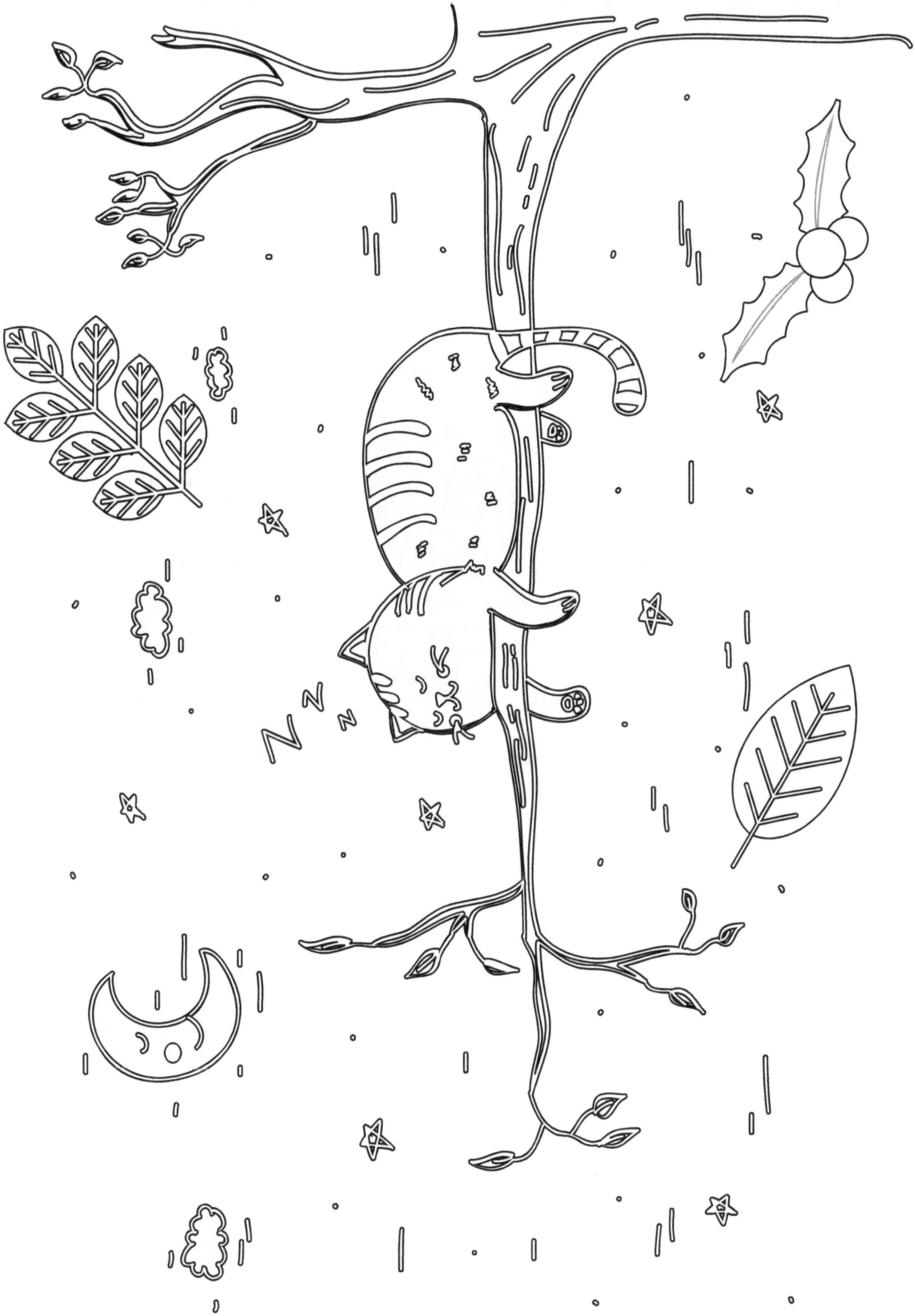

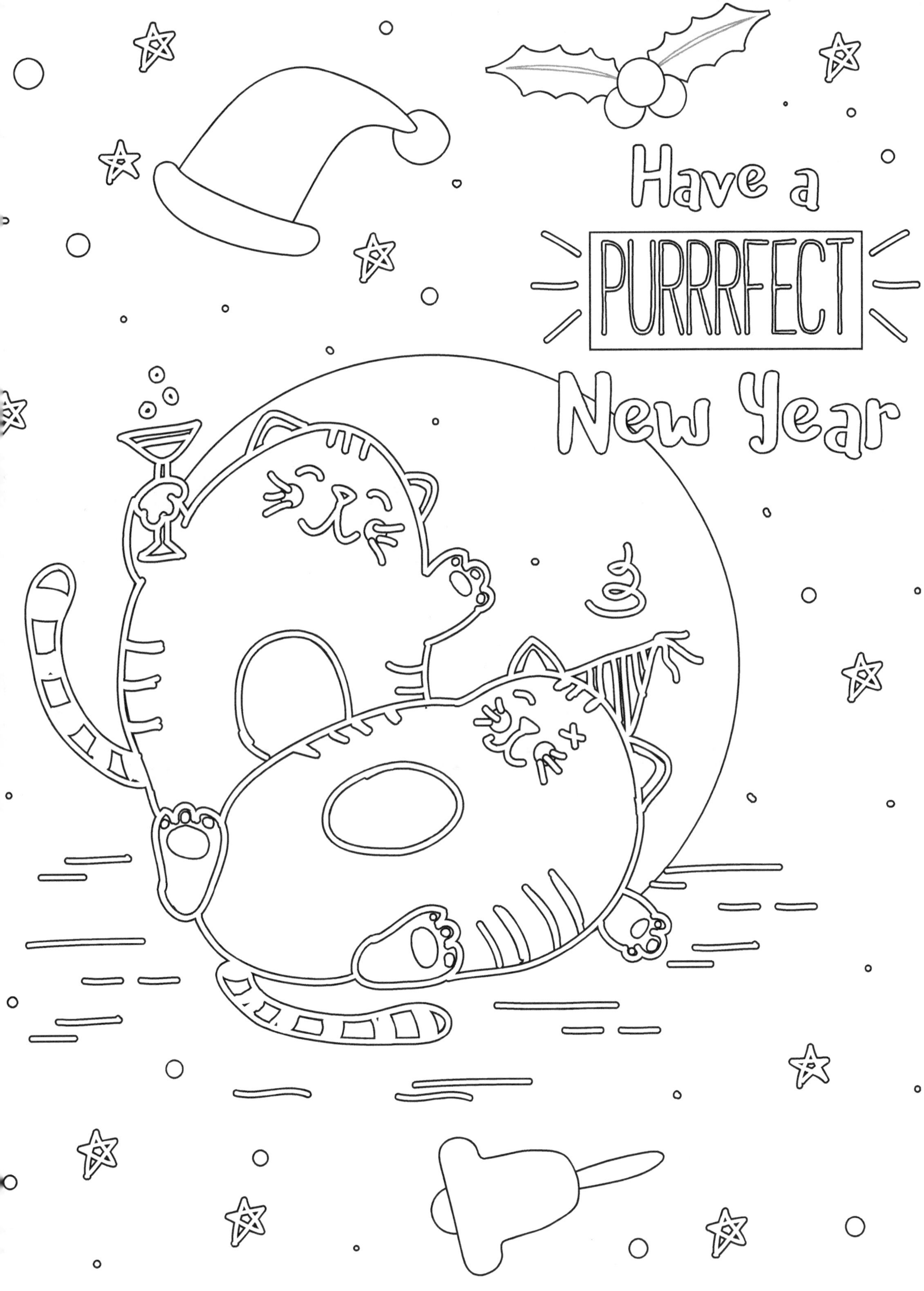
Have a
PURRRFECT
New Year

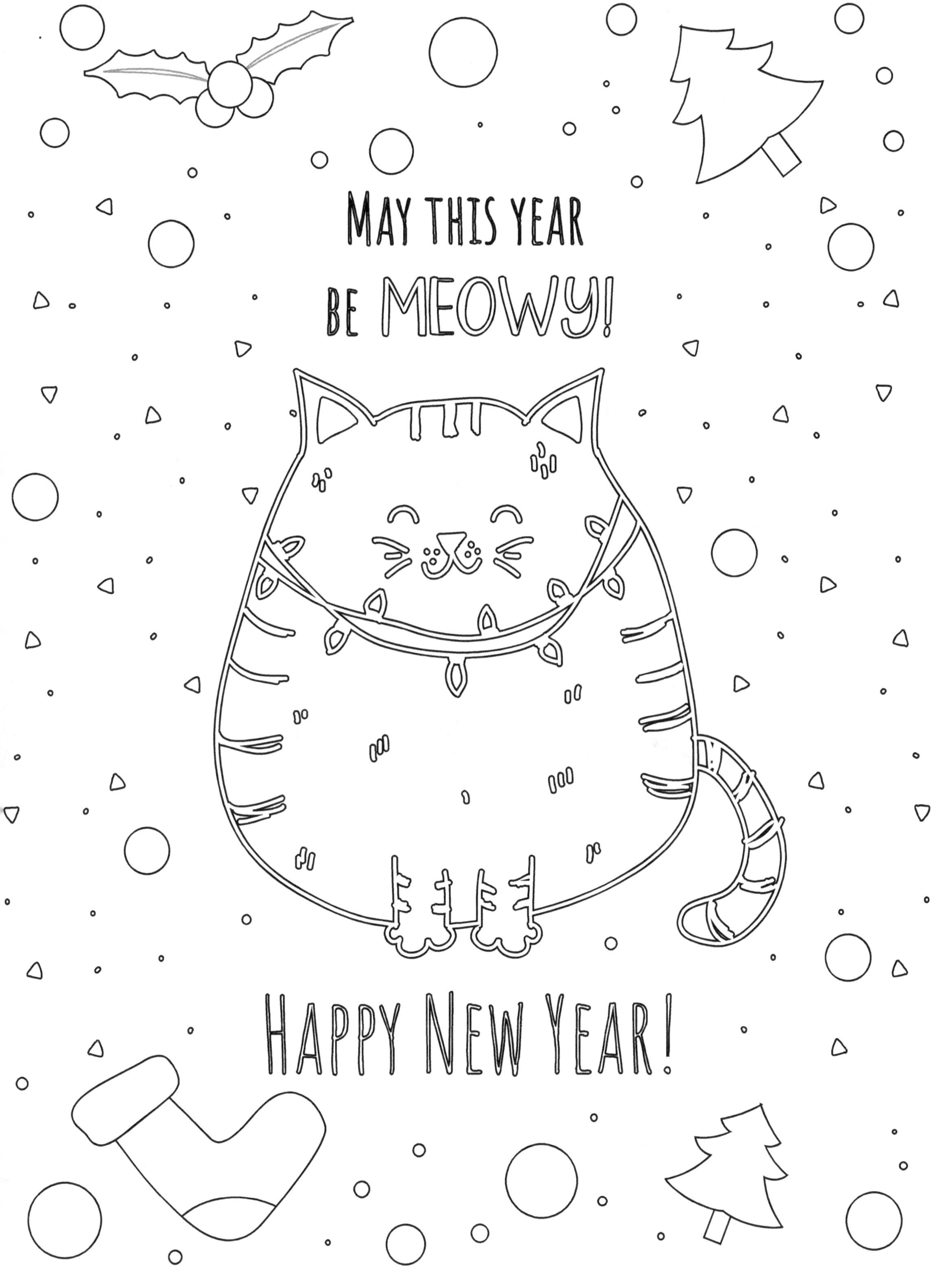
MAY THIS YEAR BE MEOWY!
HAPPY NEW YEAR!

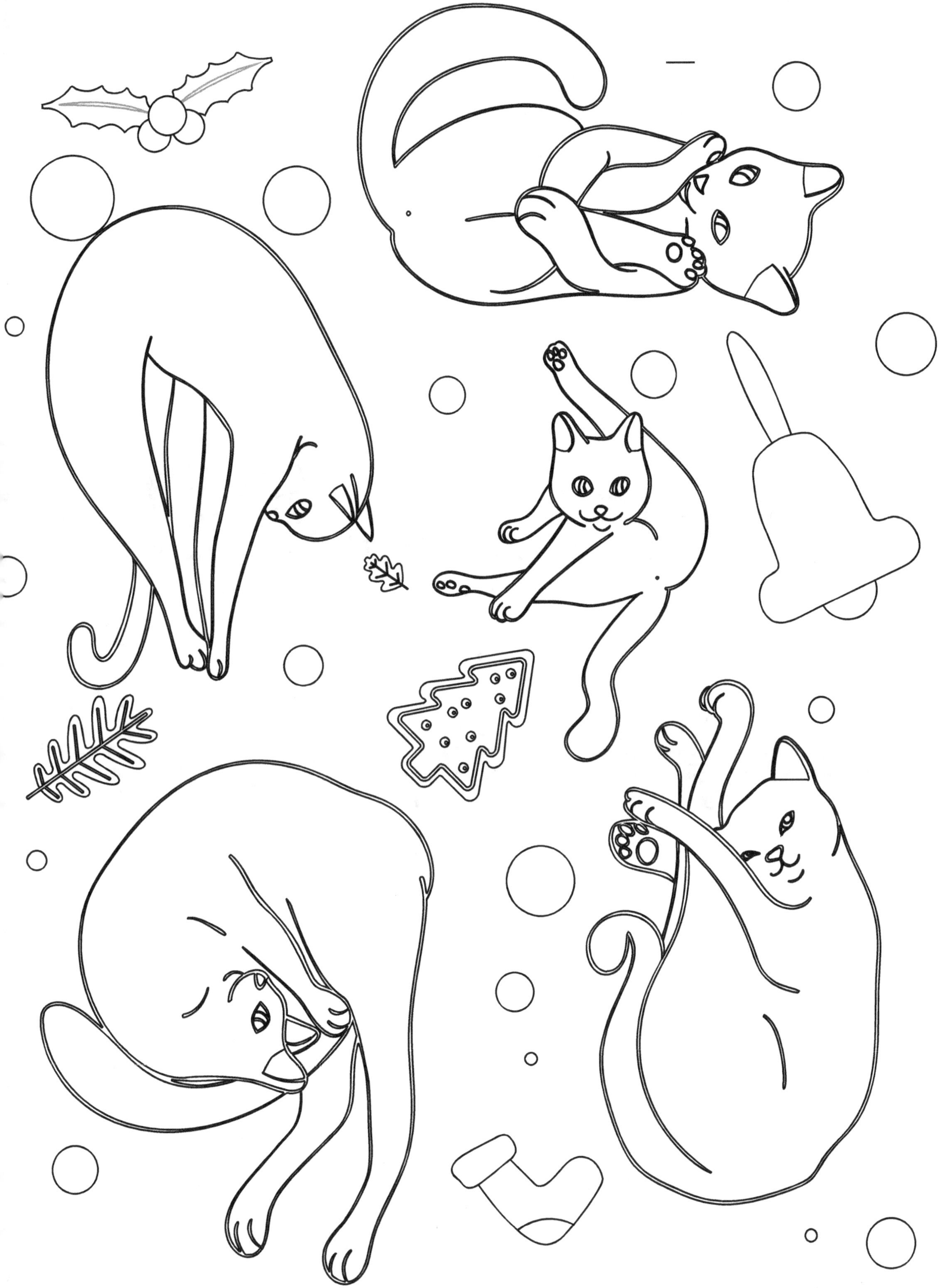

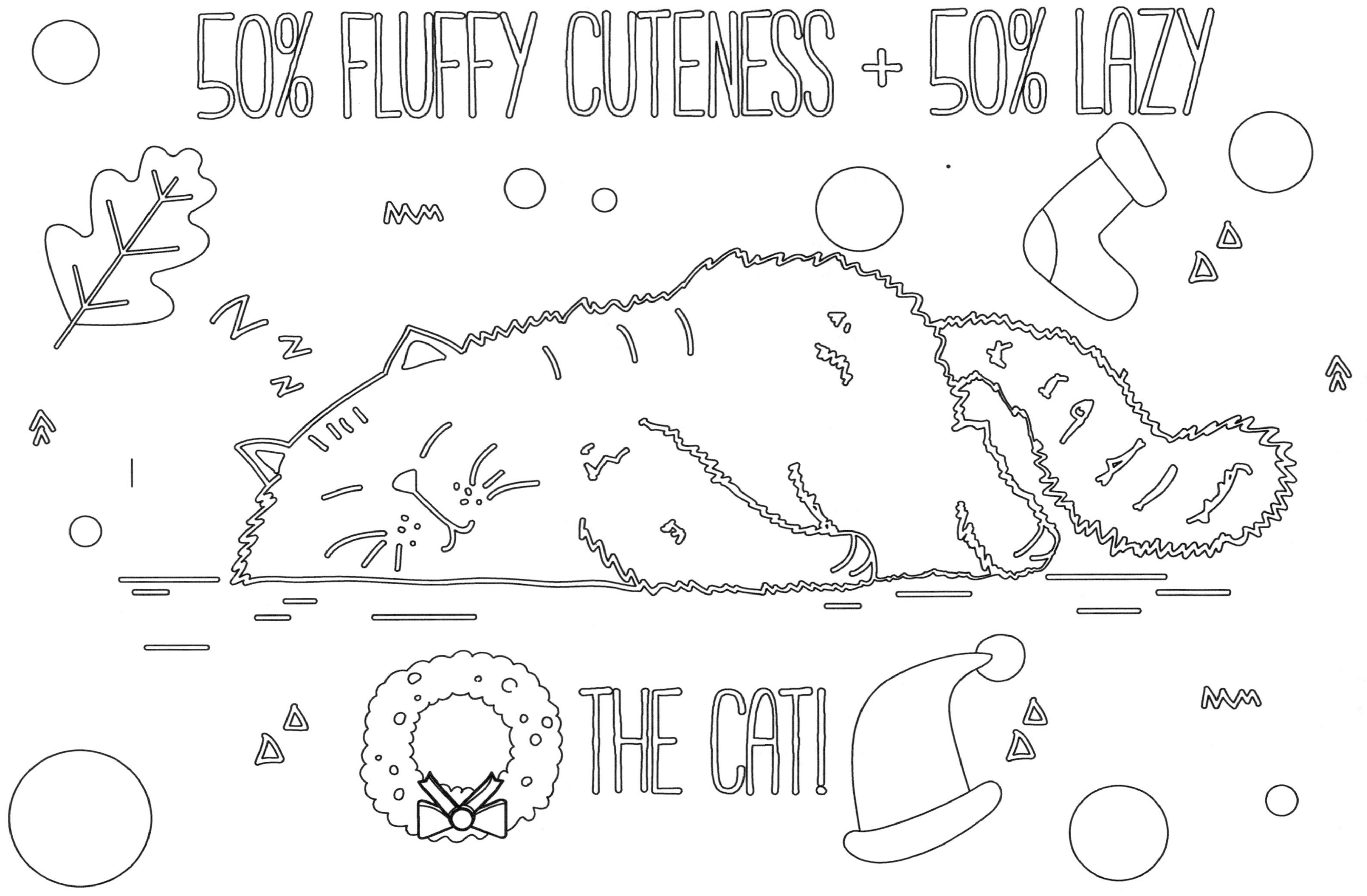
50% FLUFFY CUTENESS + 50% LAZY
THE CAT!

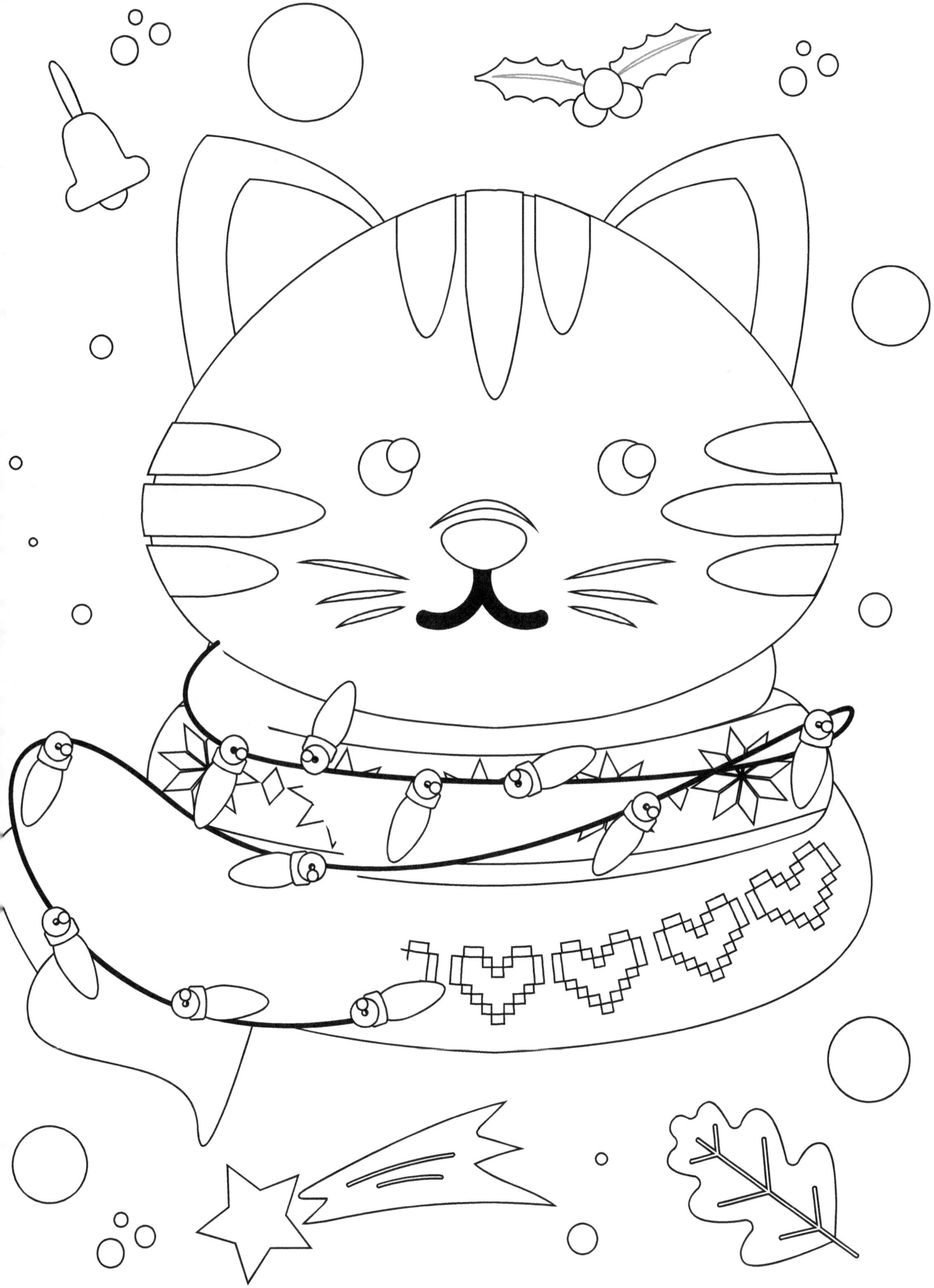

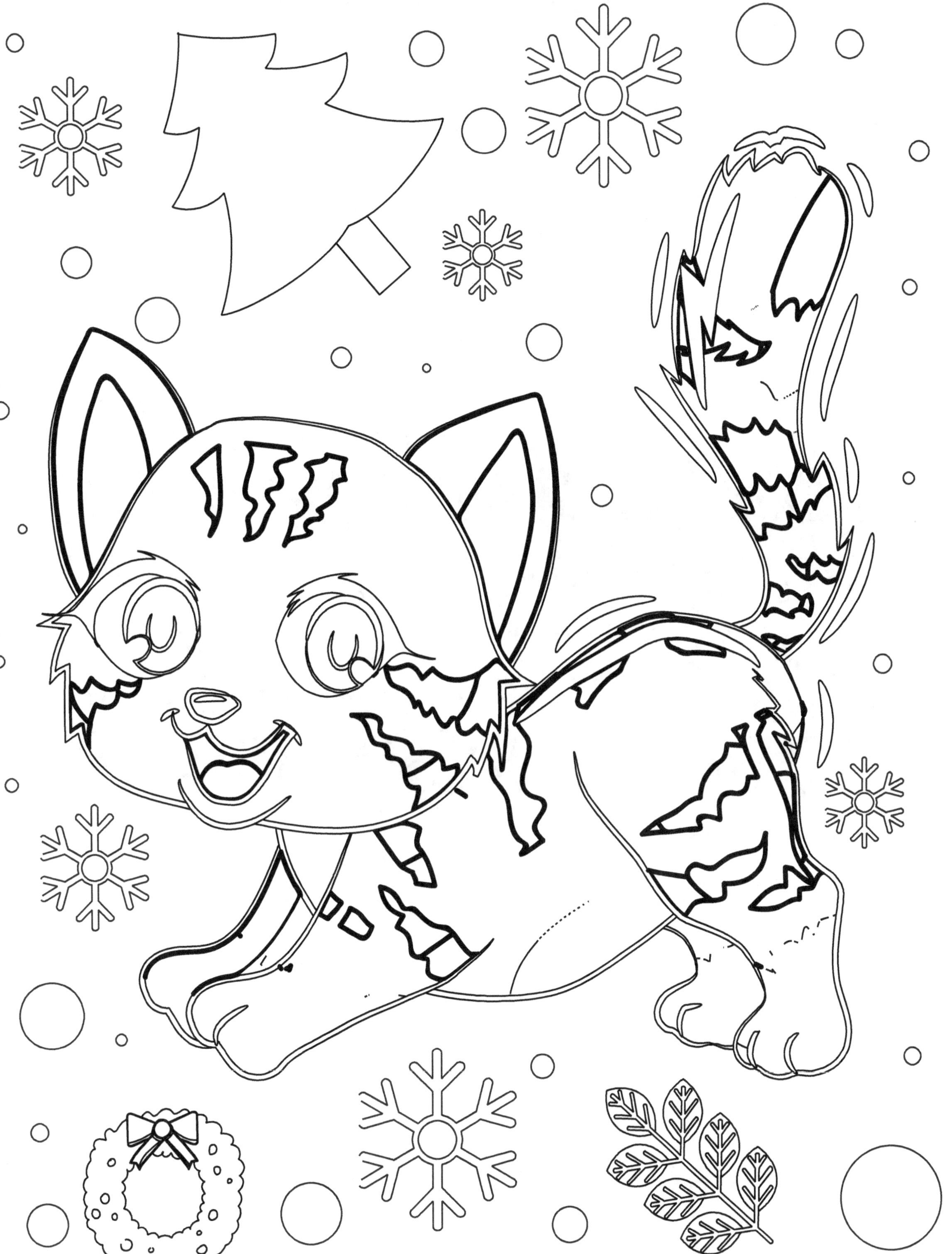

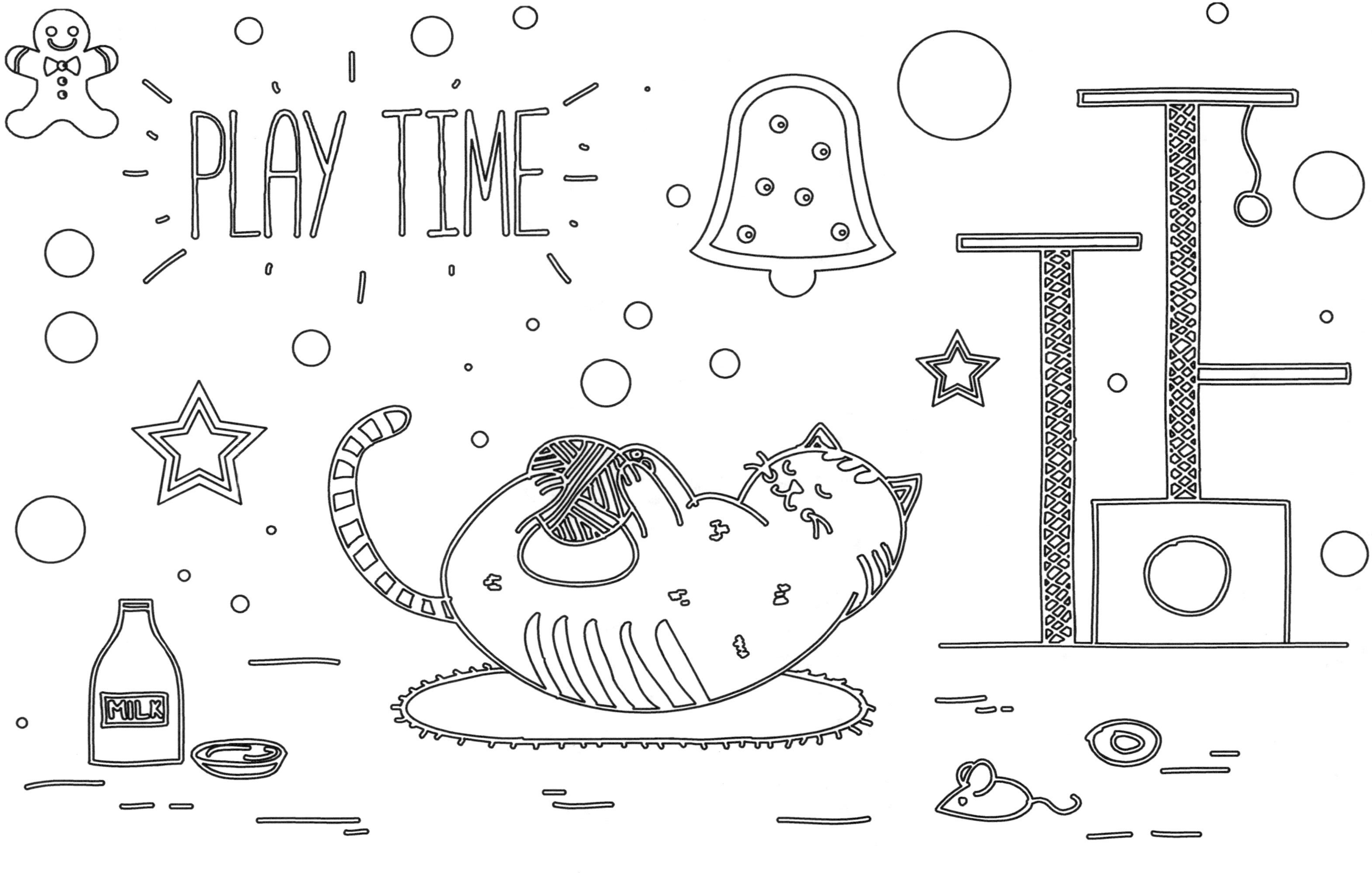
PLAY TIME
MILK

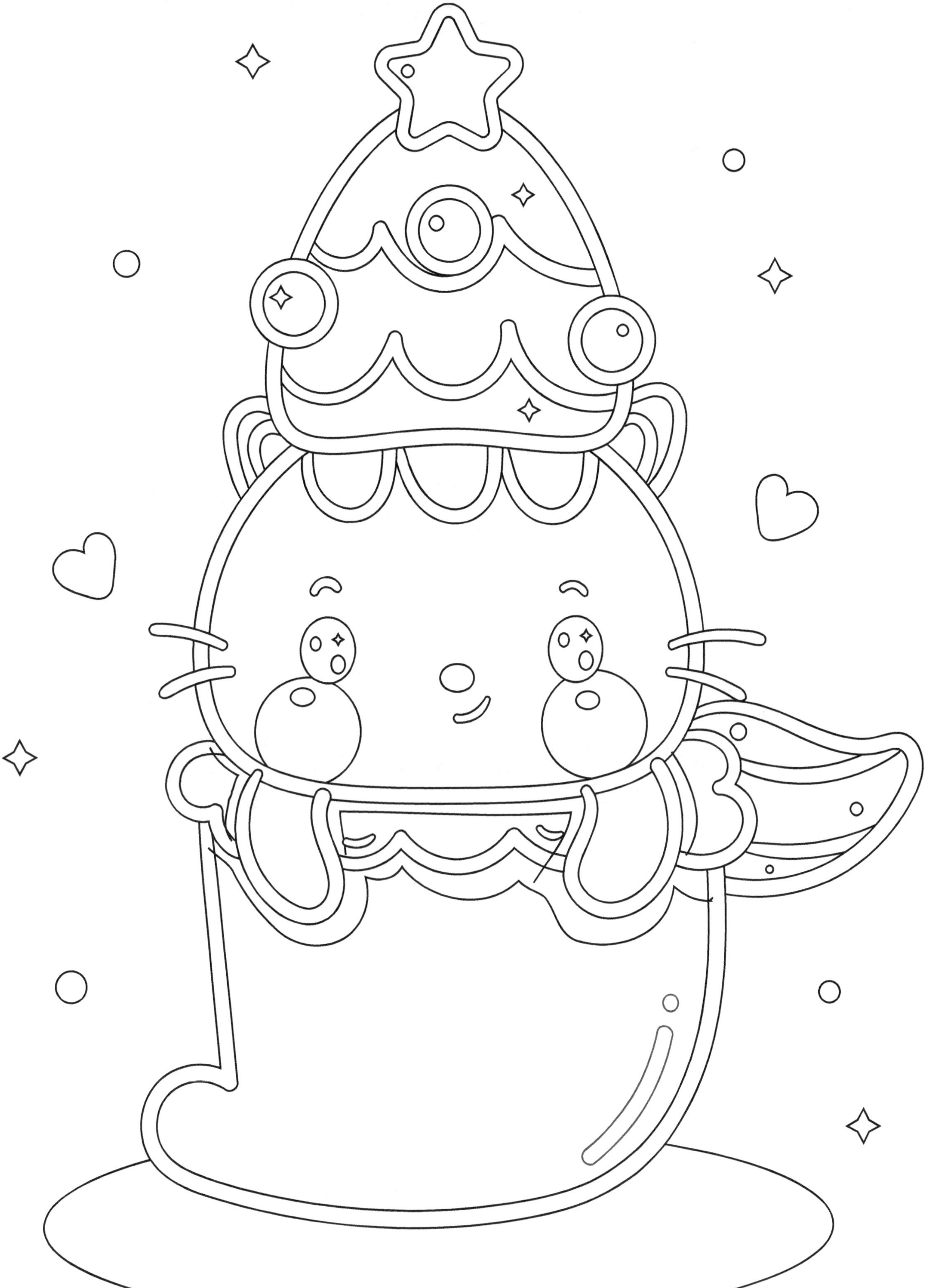

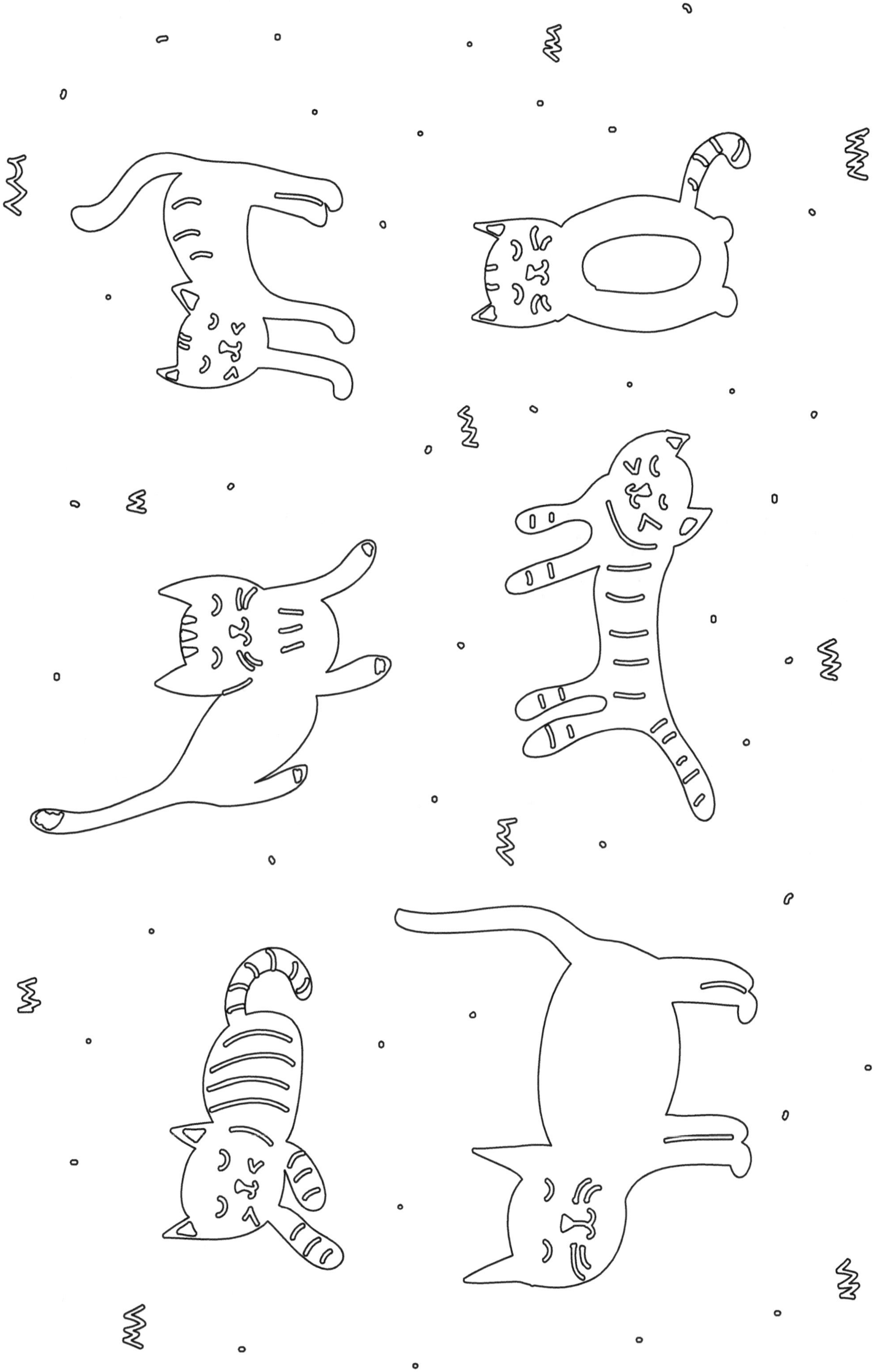

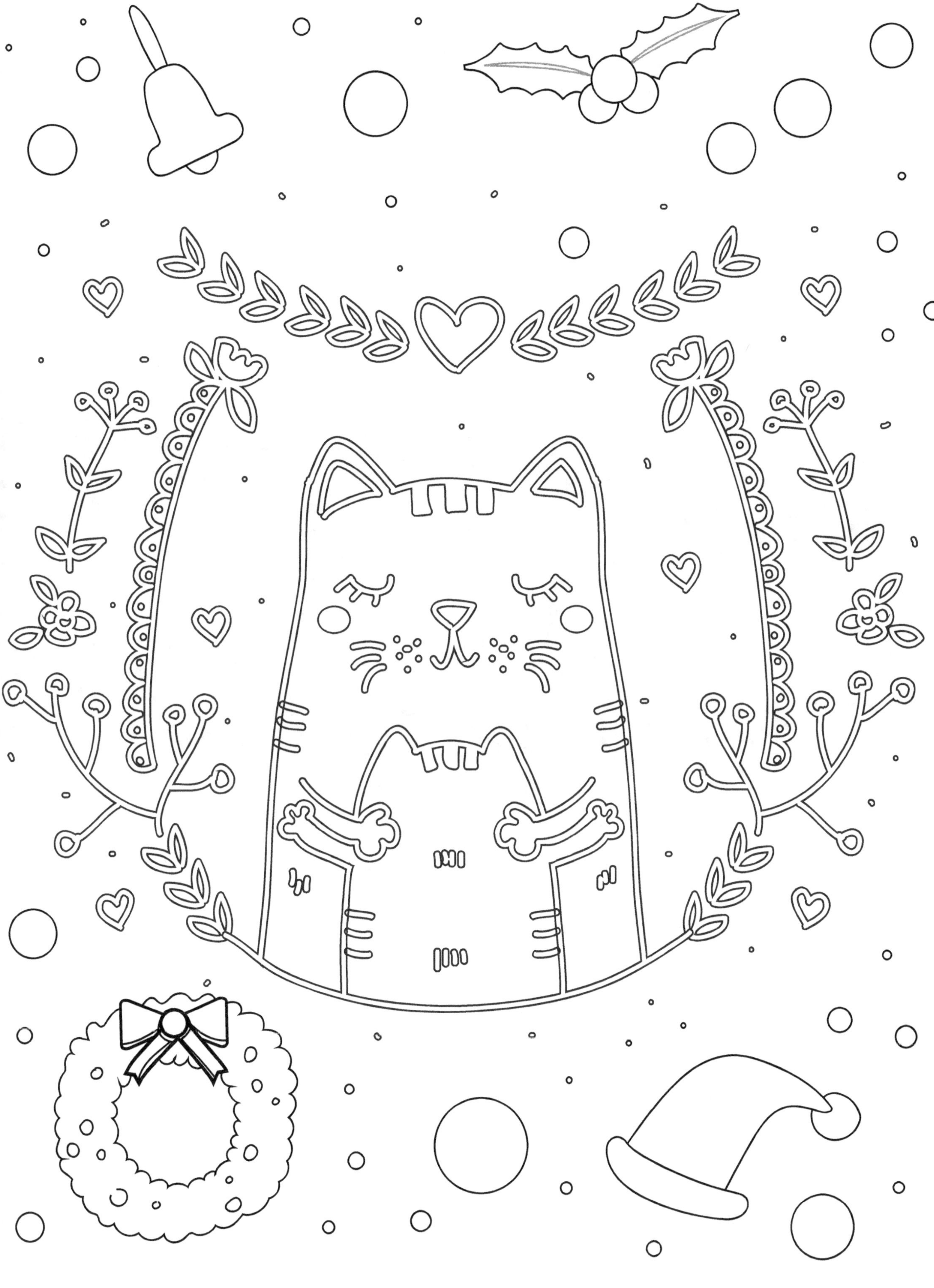

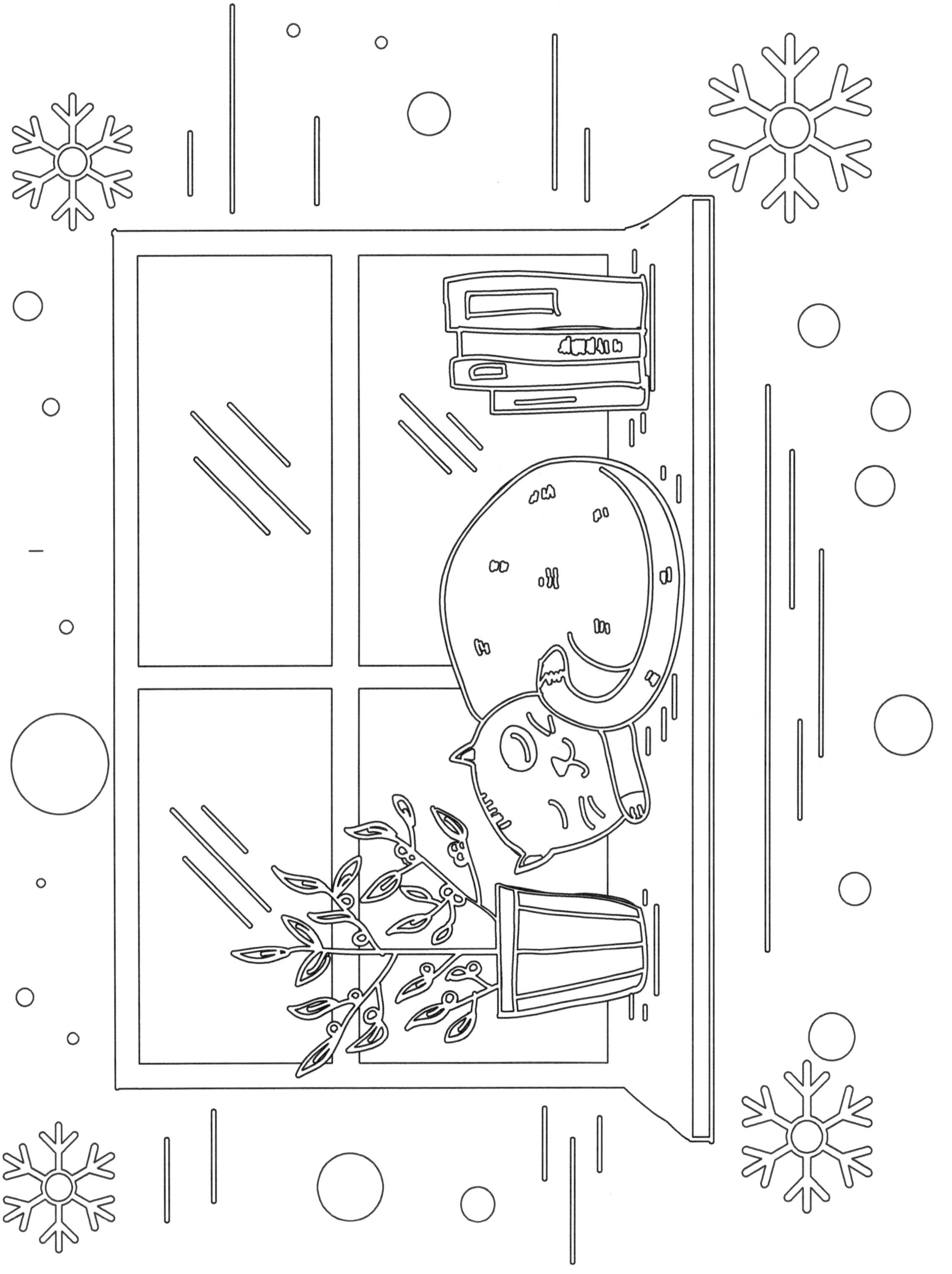

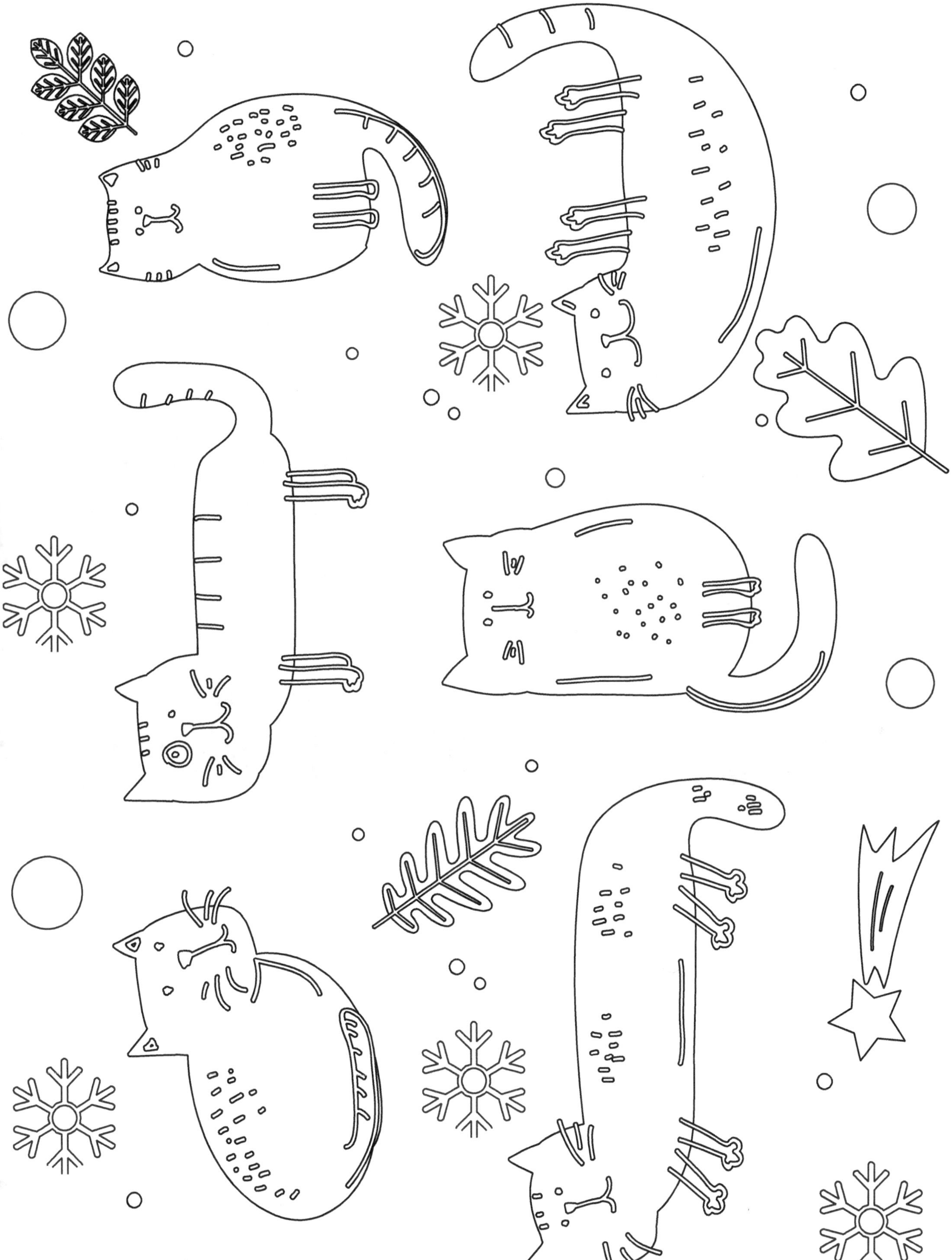

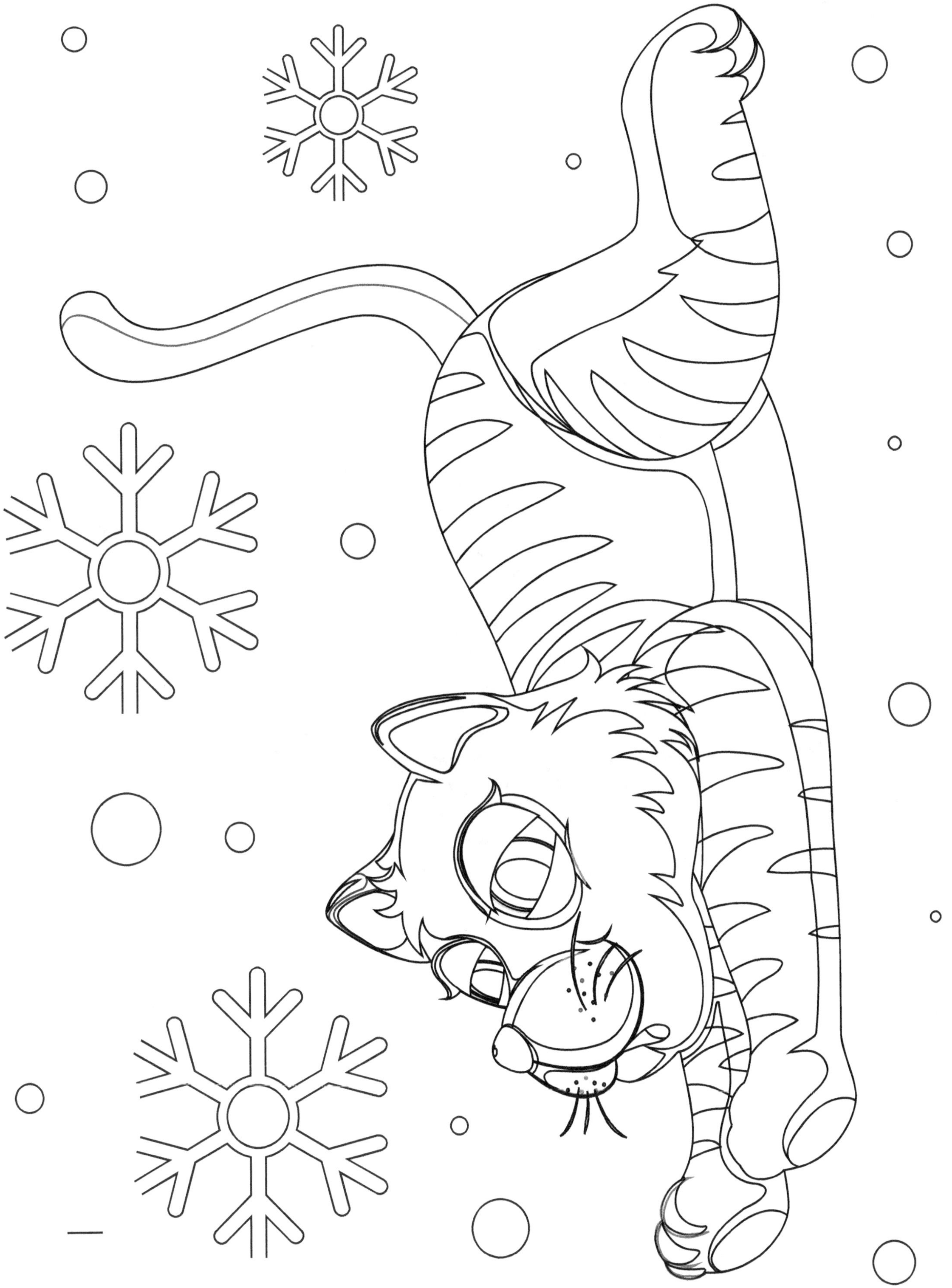

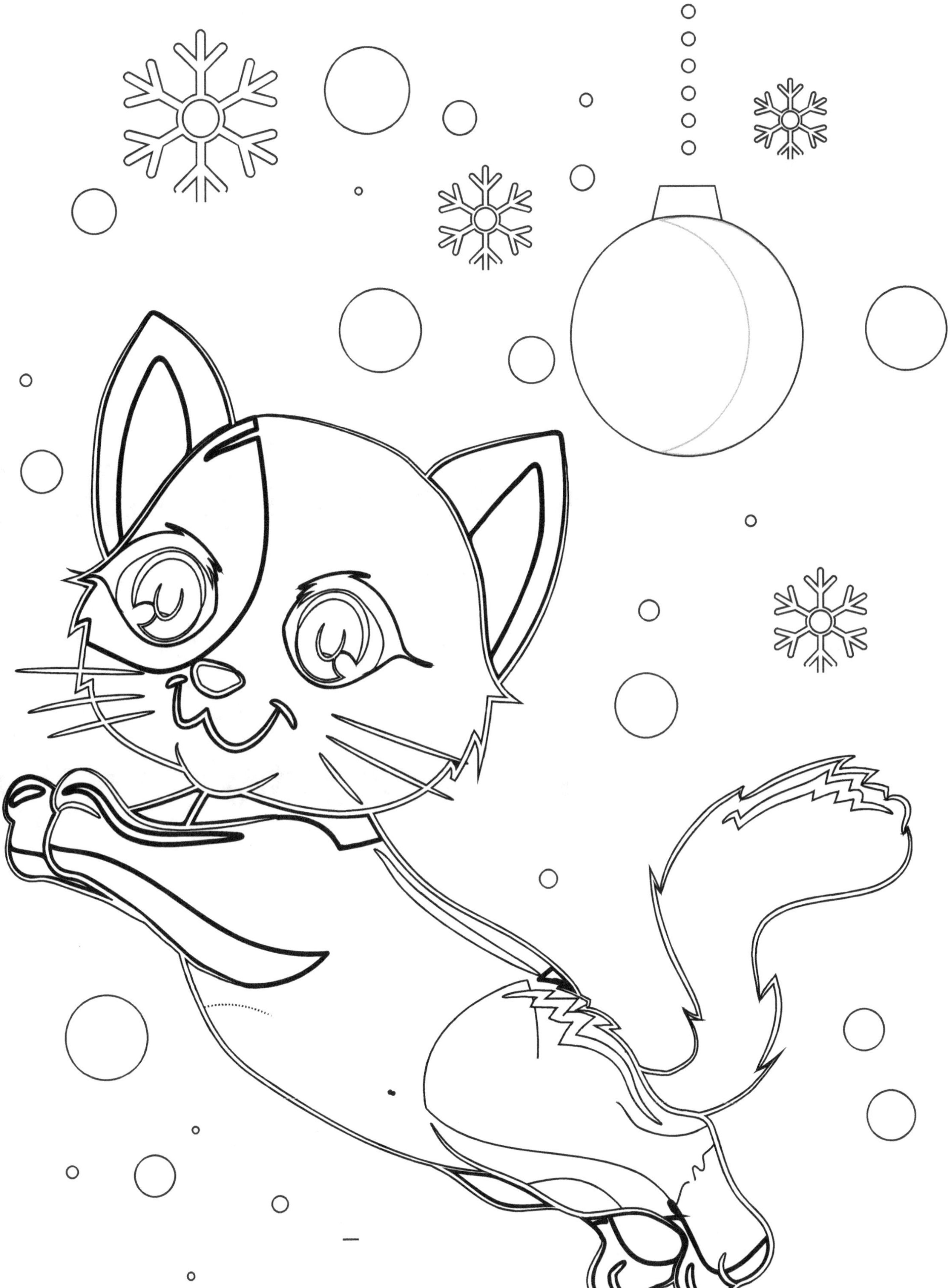

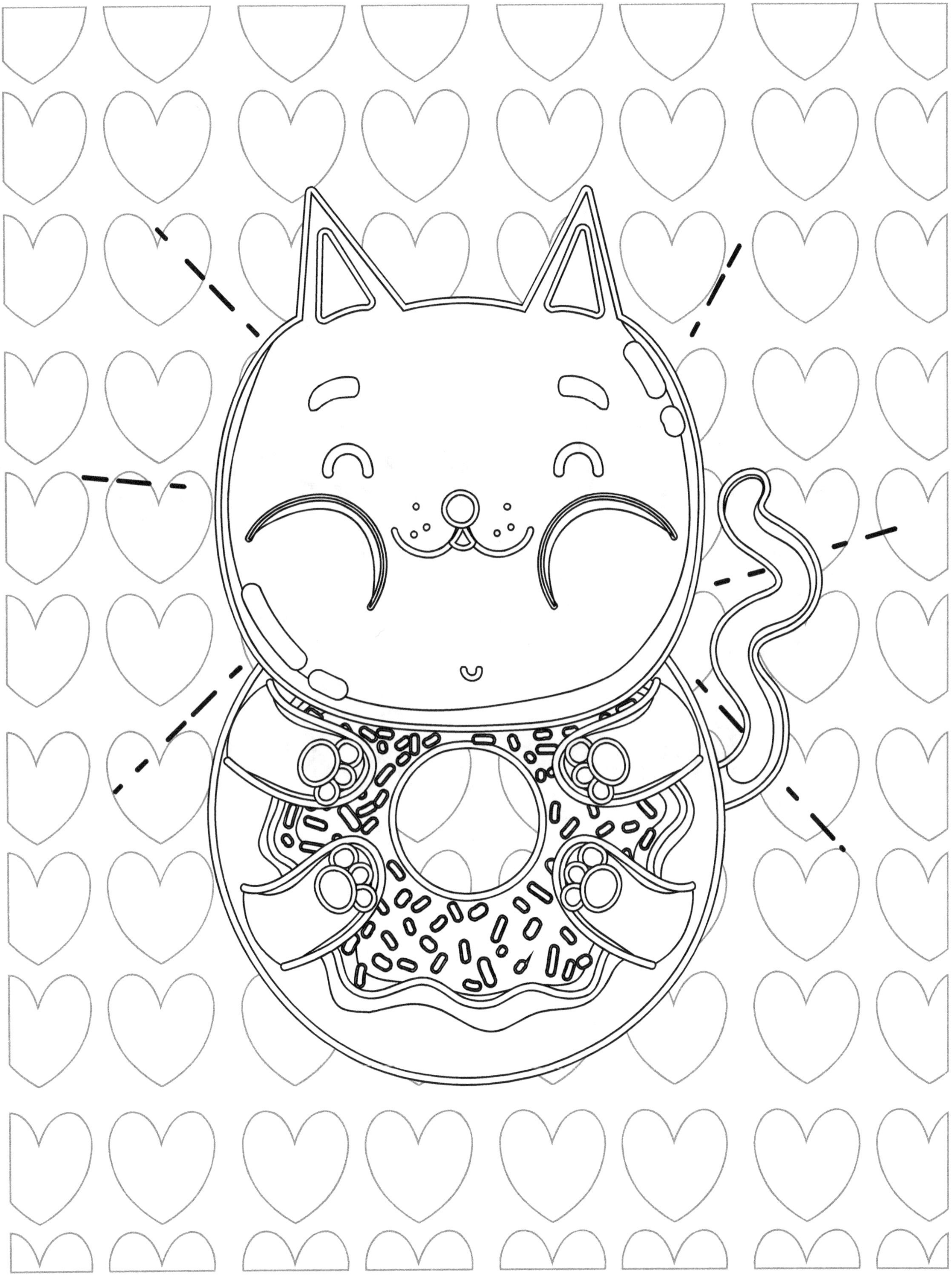

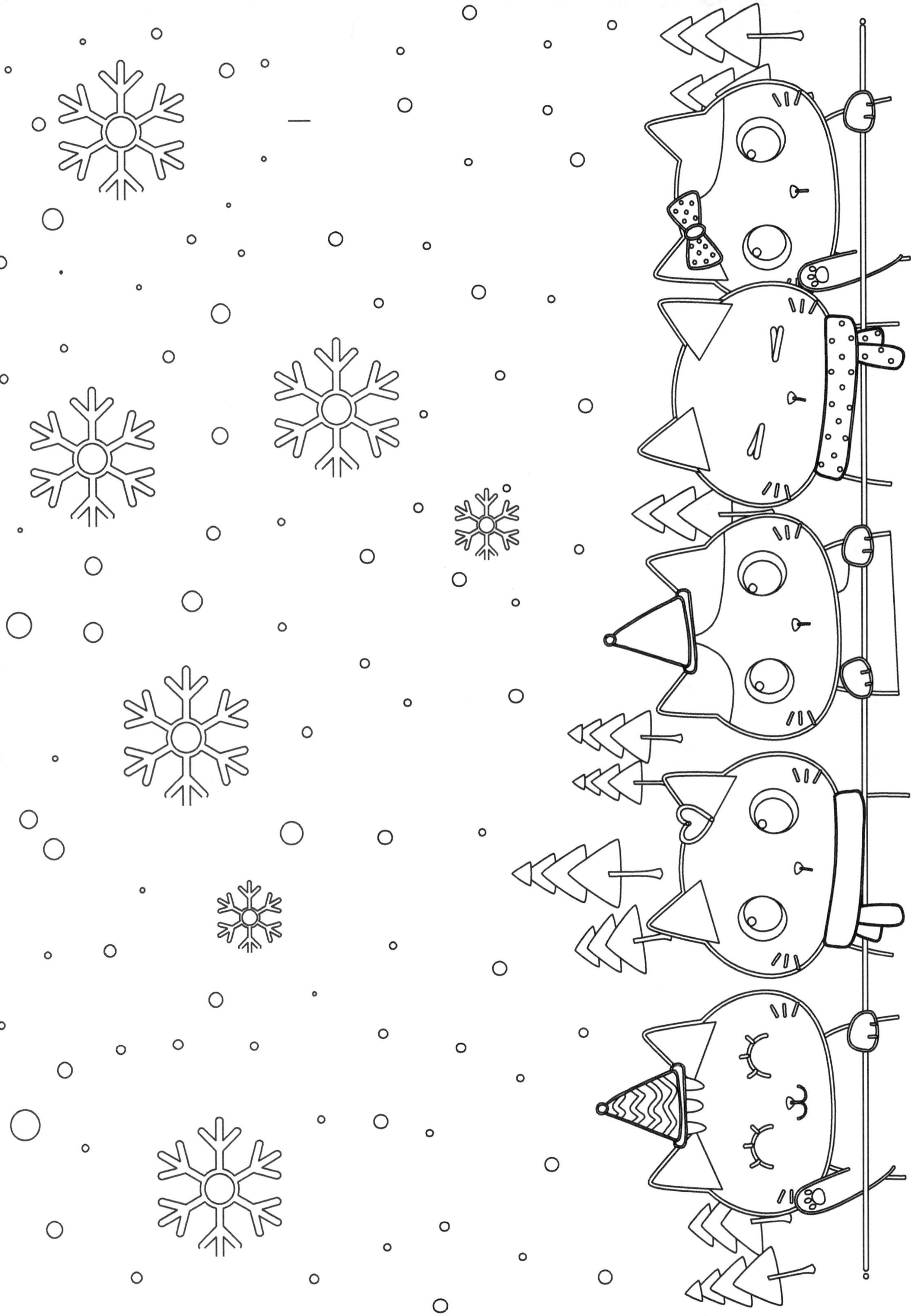

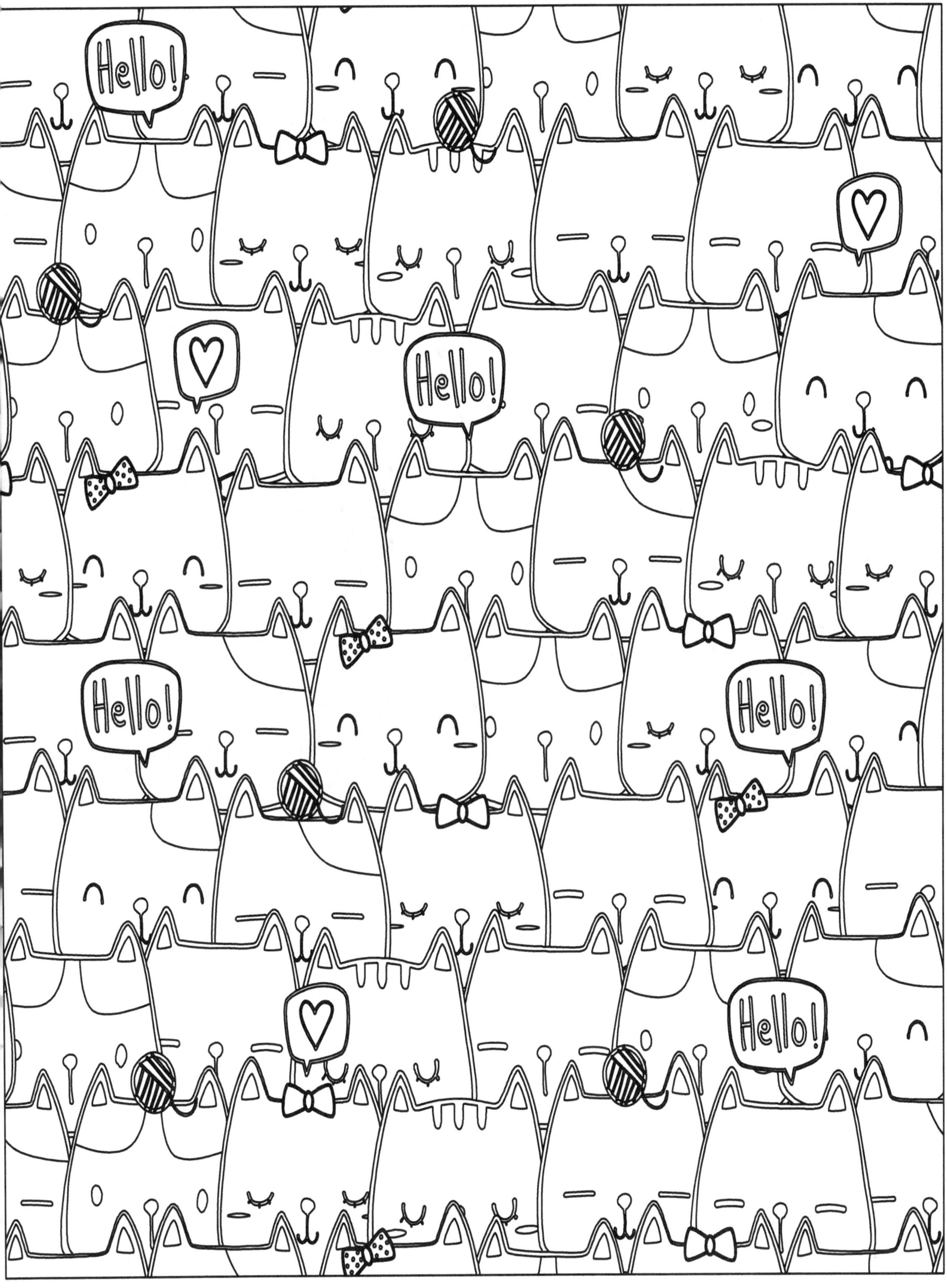
Hello!
Hello!
Hello!
Hello!
Hello!

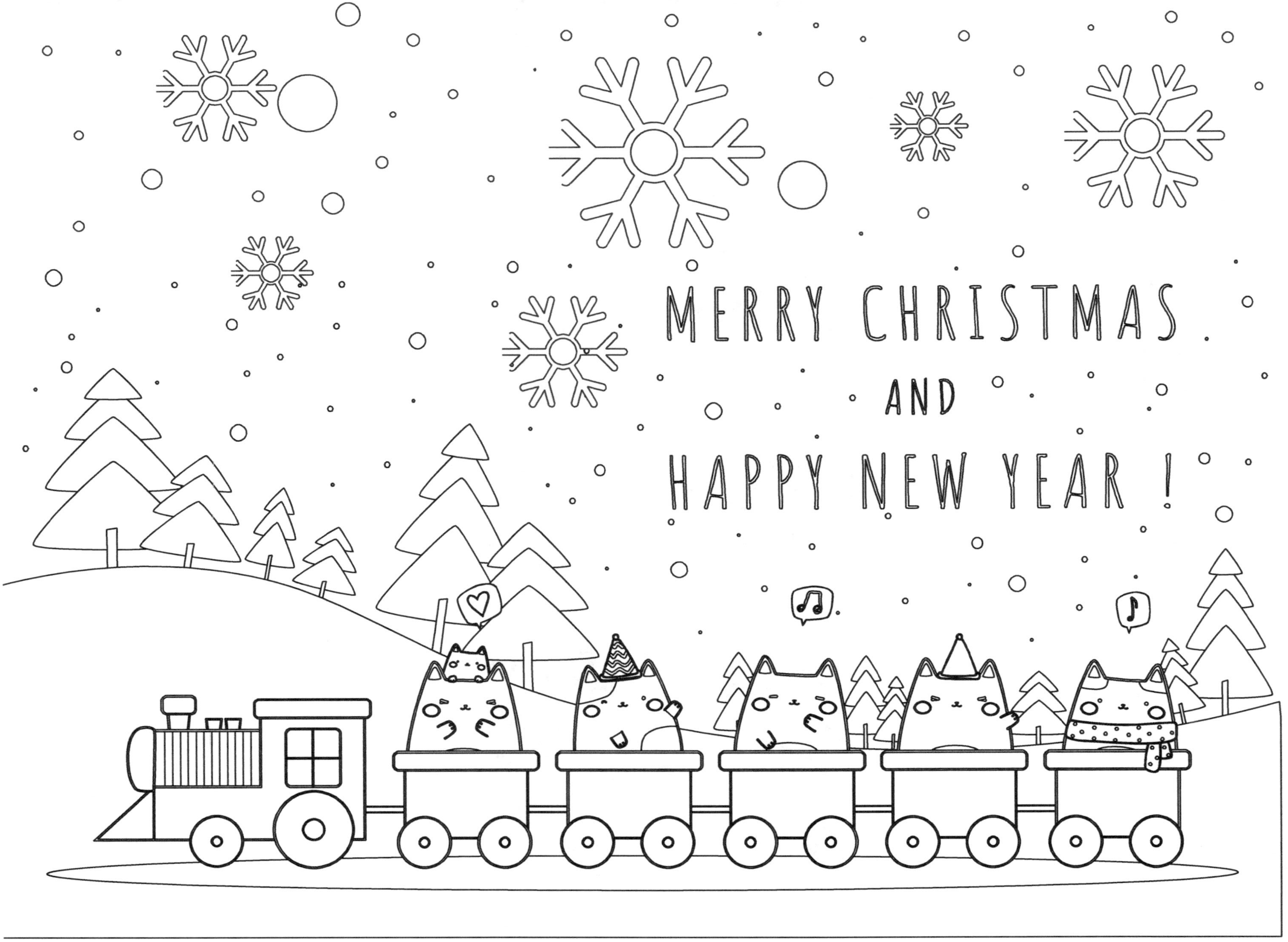
MERRY CHRISTMAS
AND
HAPPY NEW YEAR !

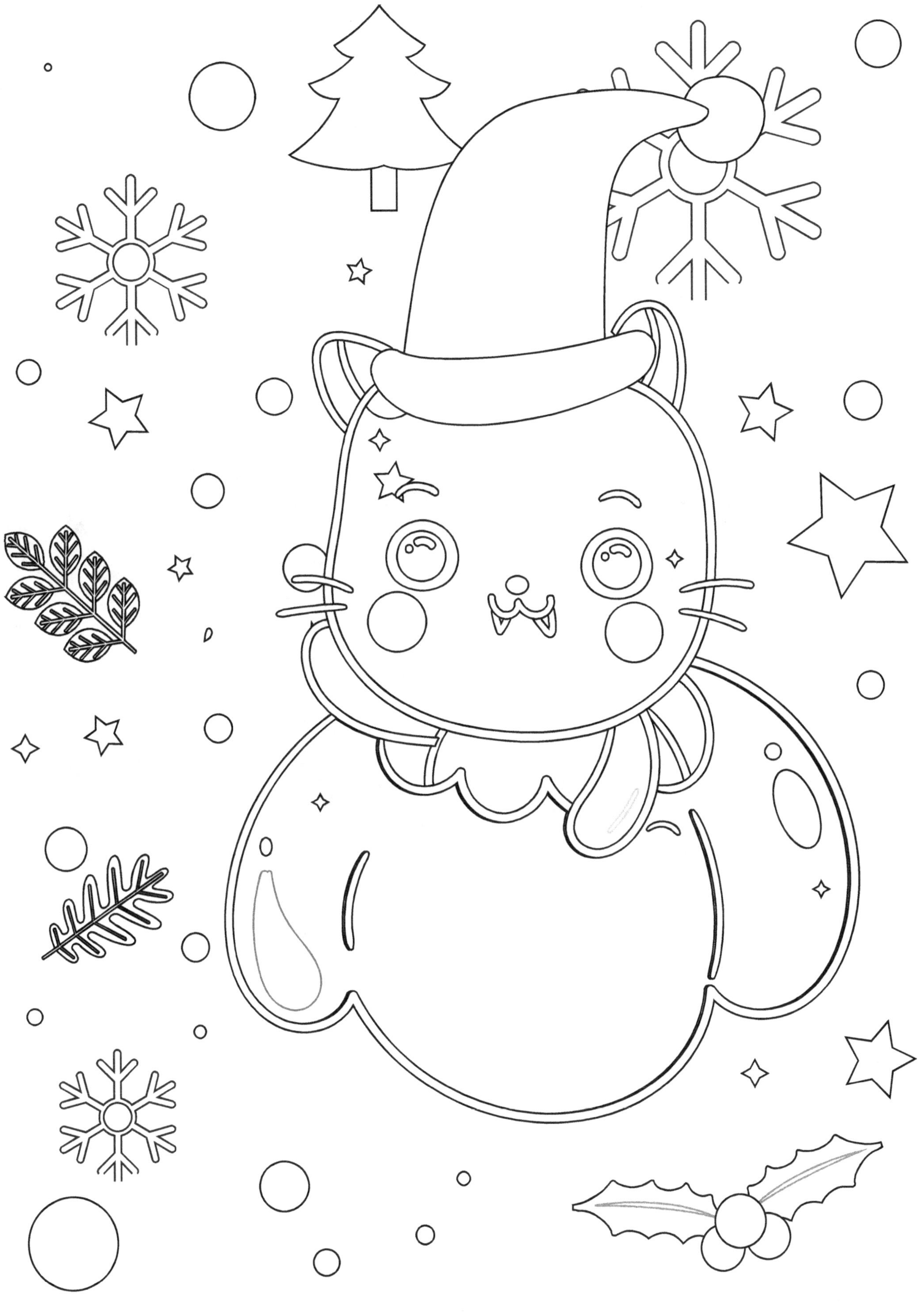

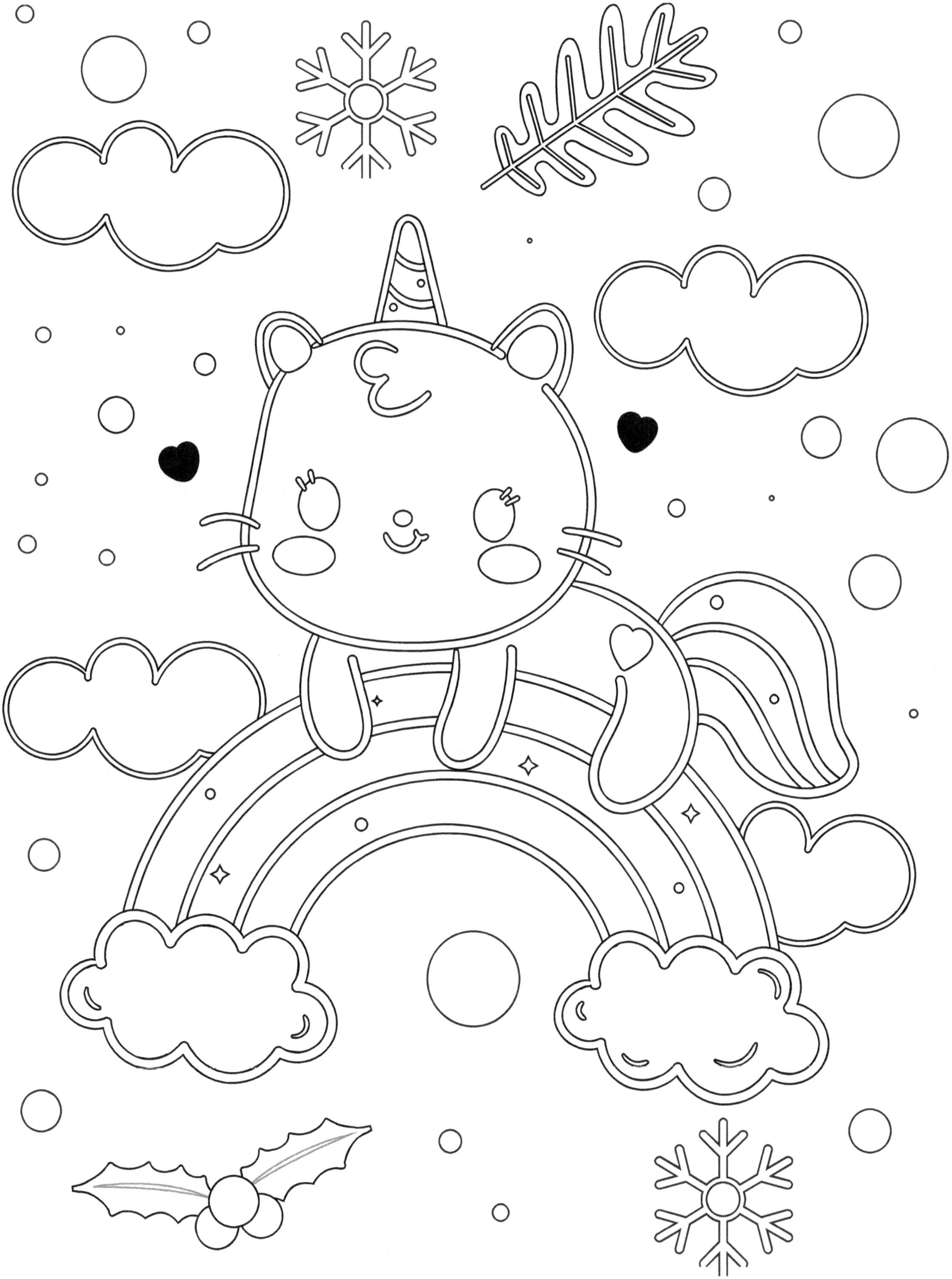

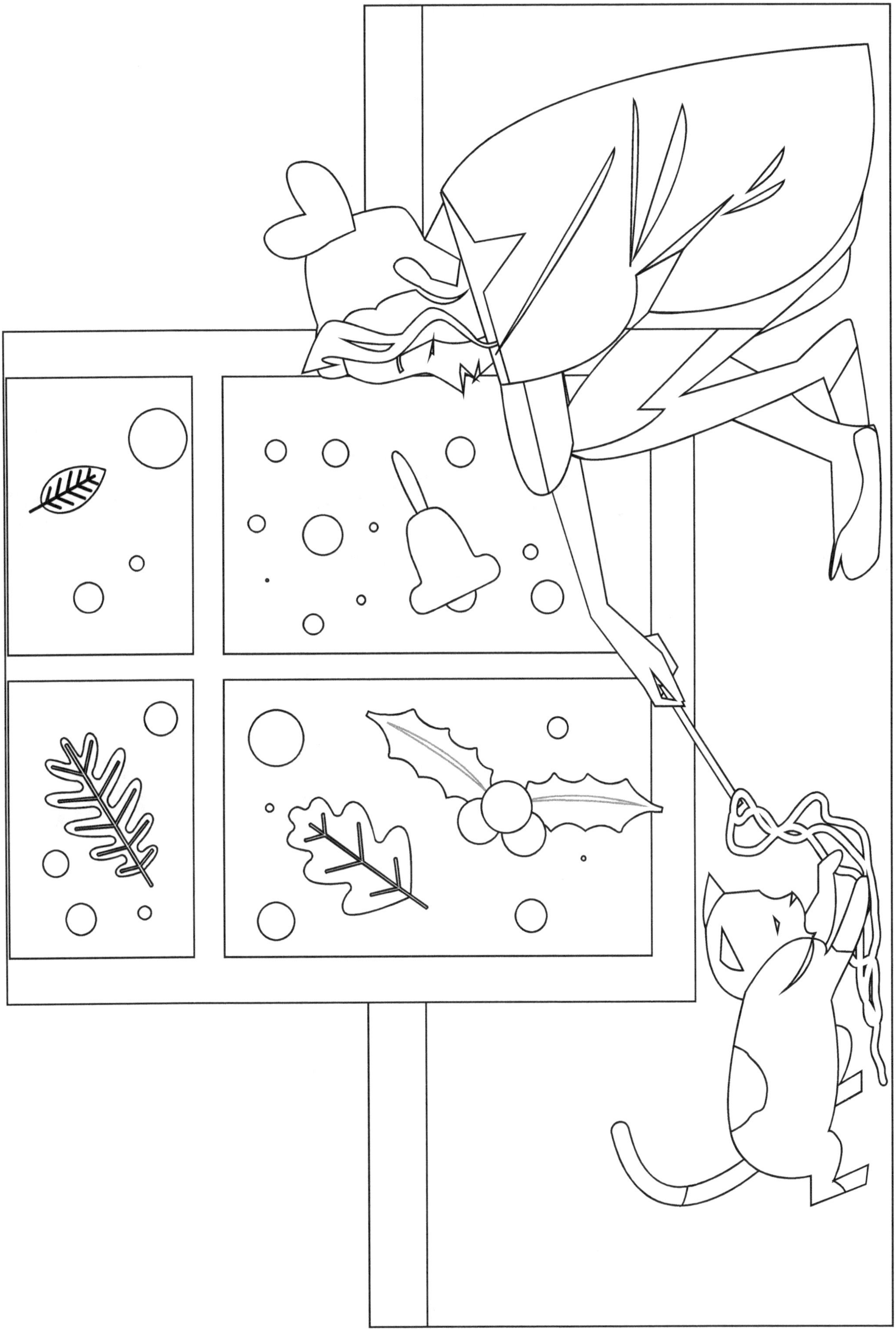

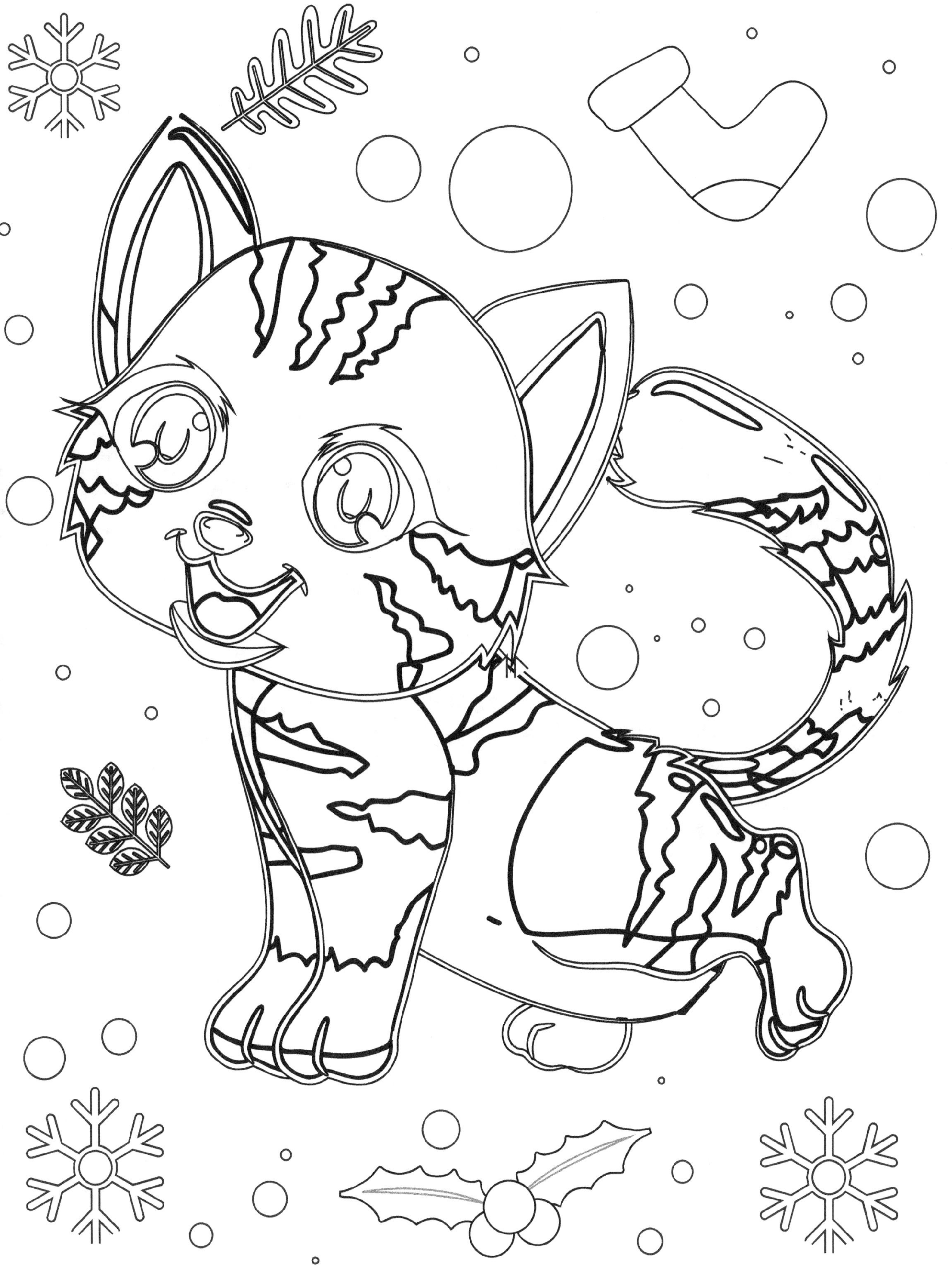

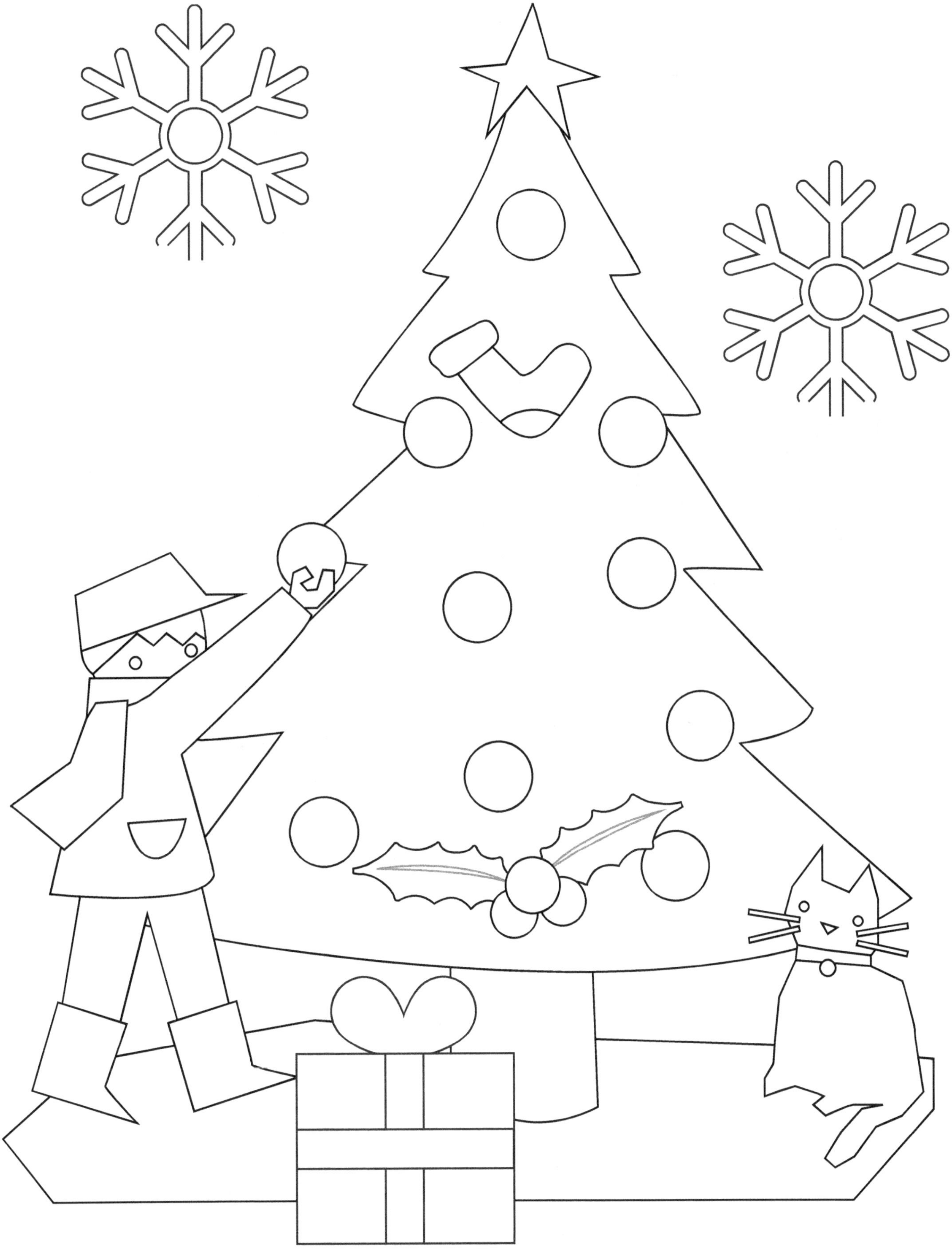

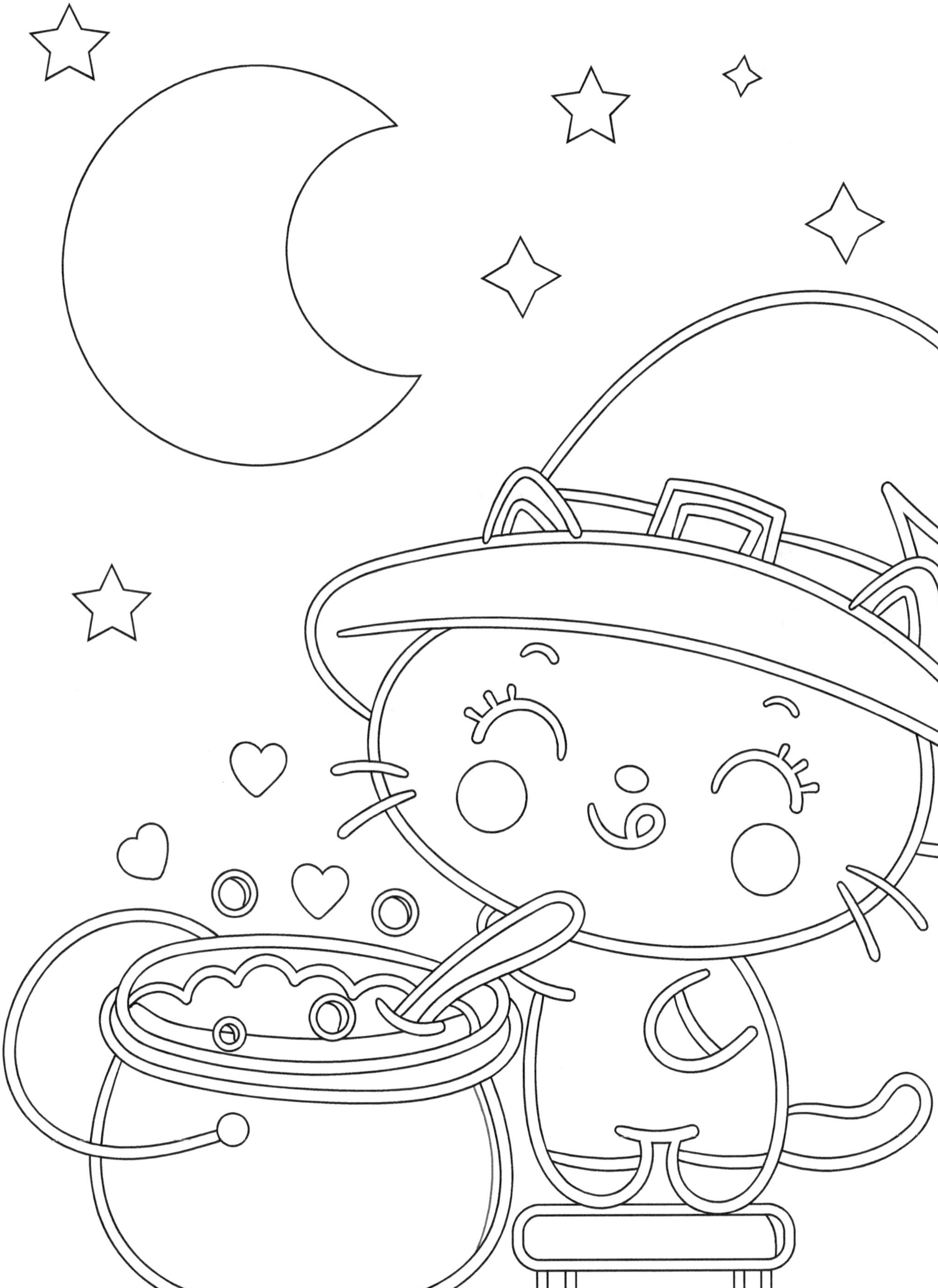

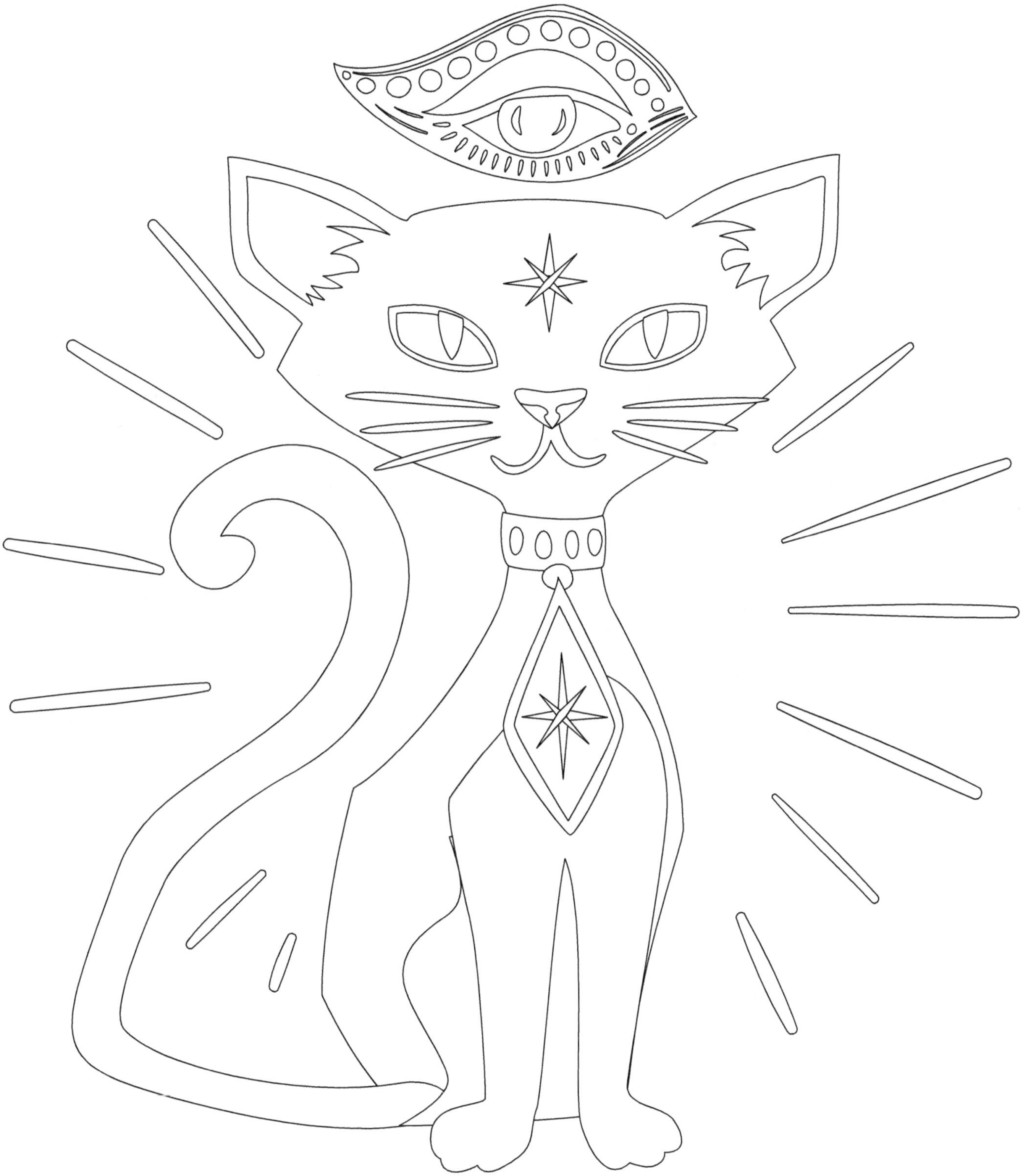

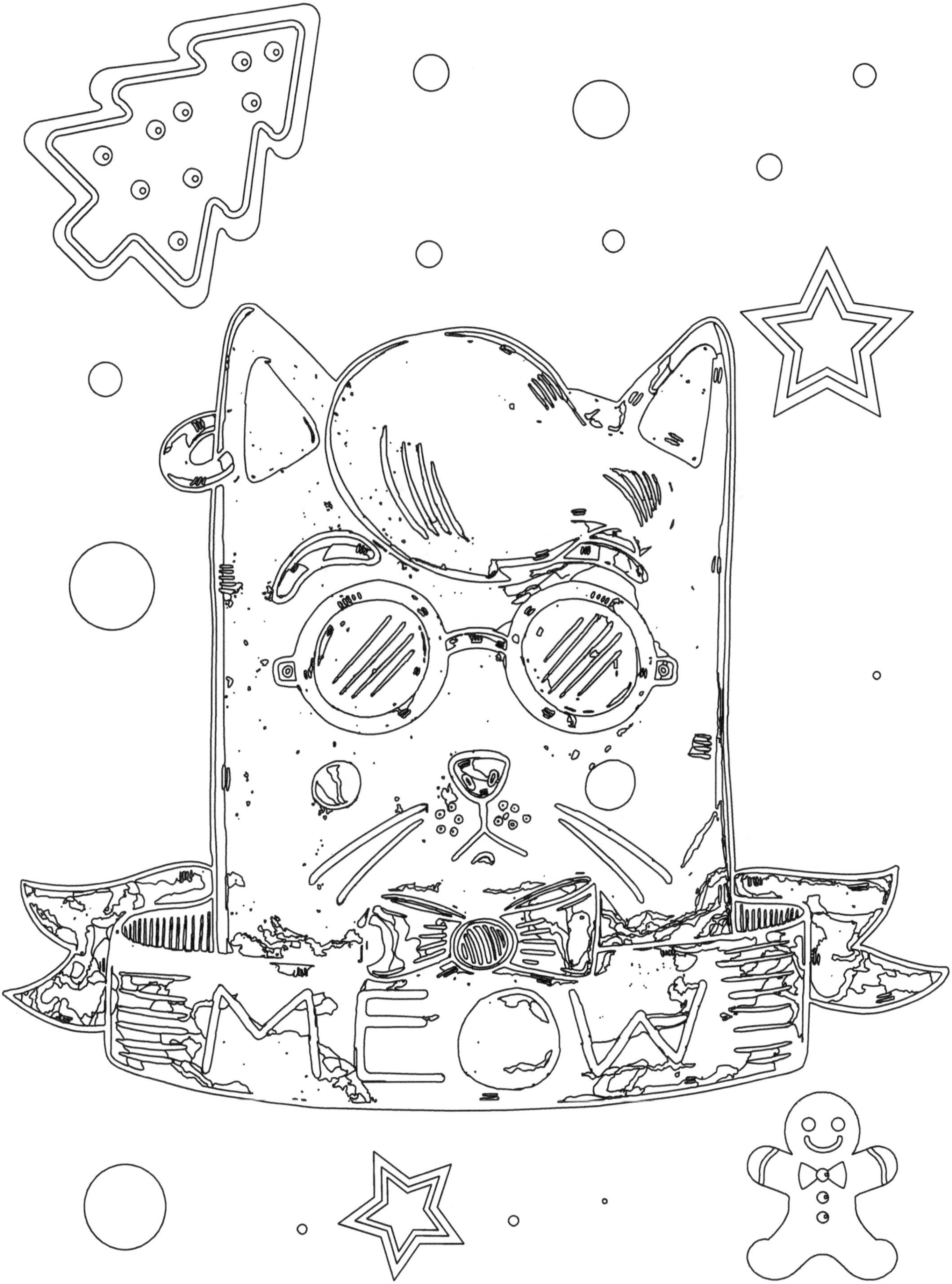
MEOW

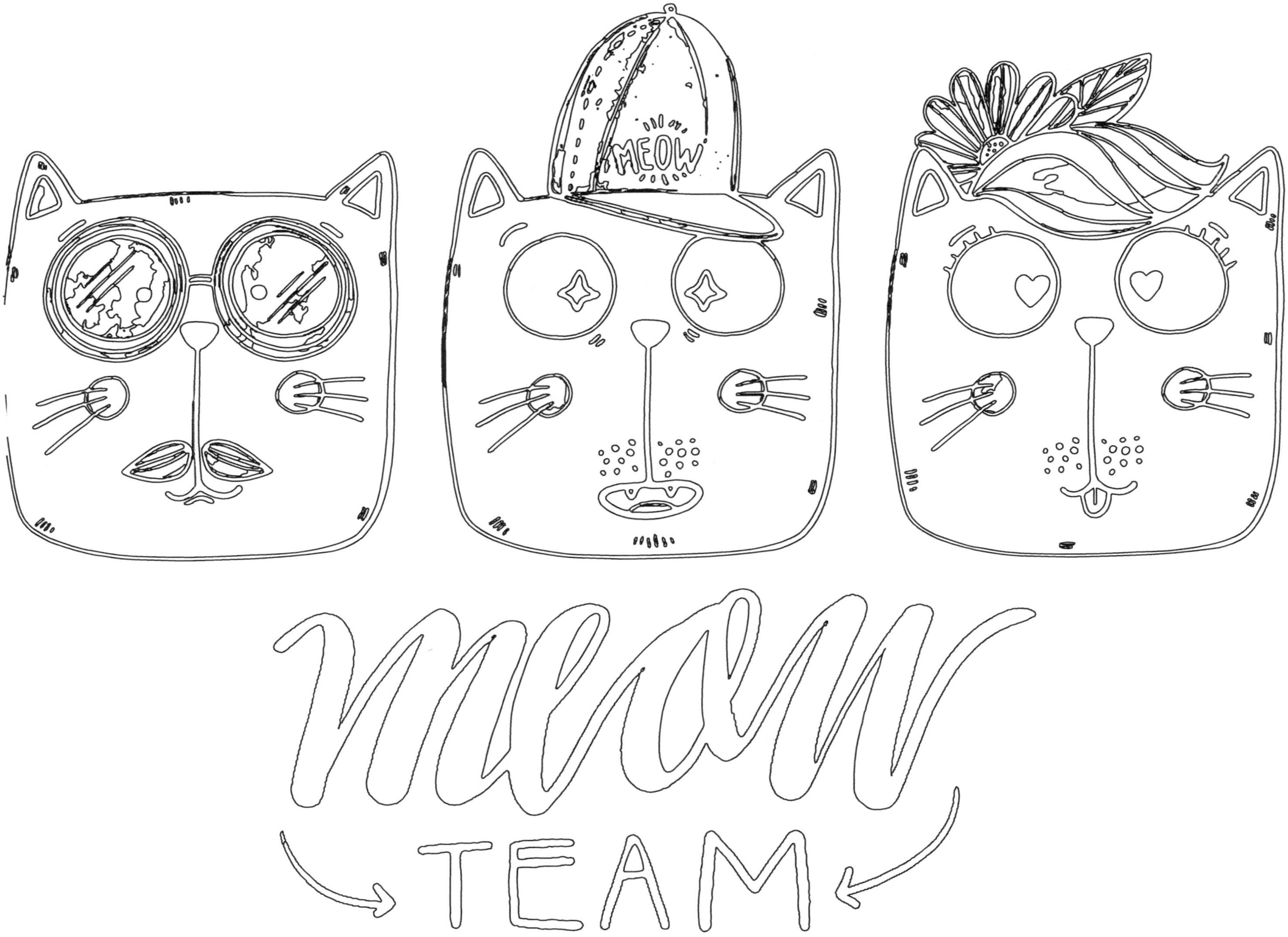
MEOW
meow
TEAM

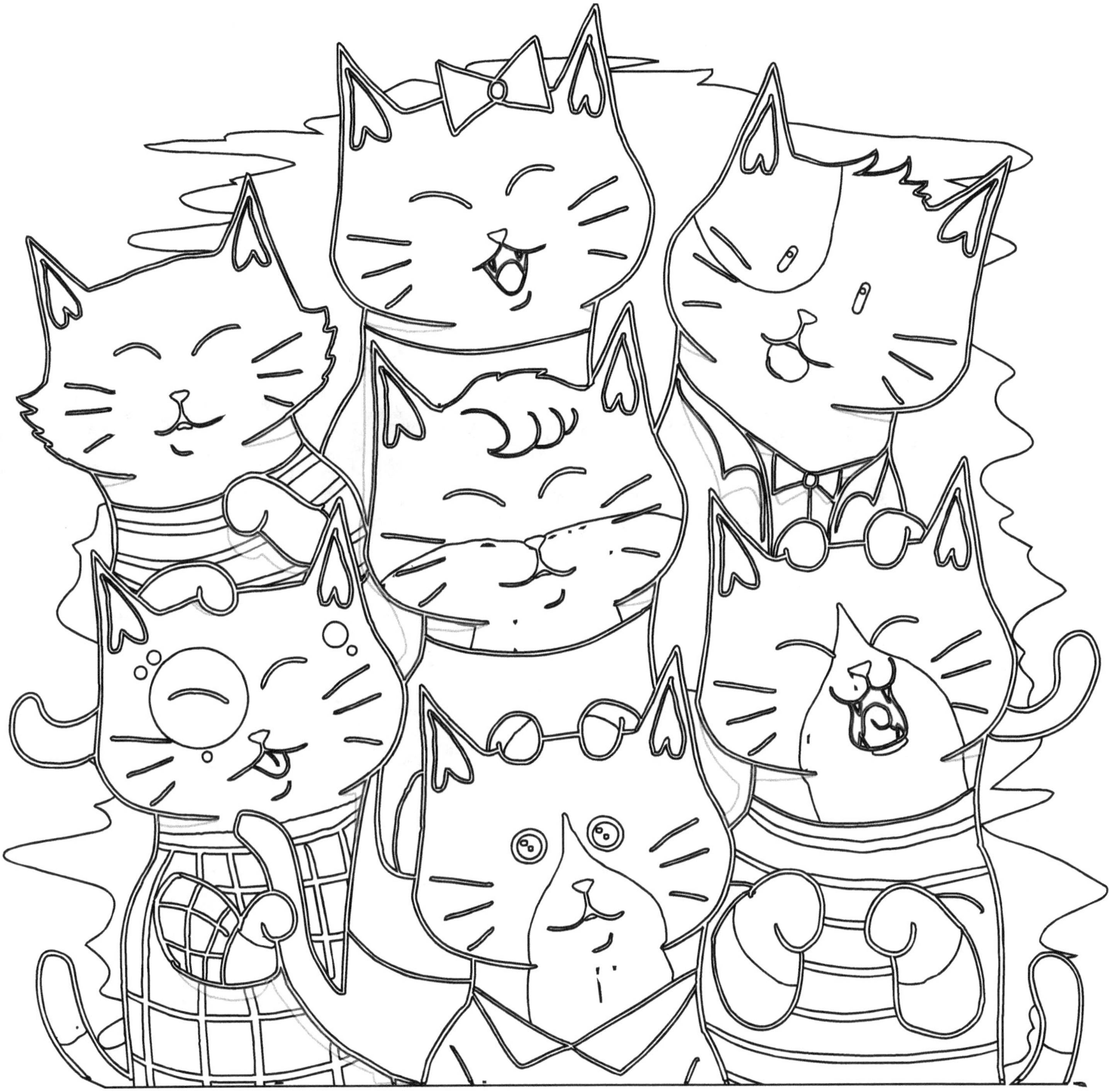

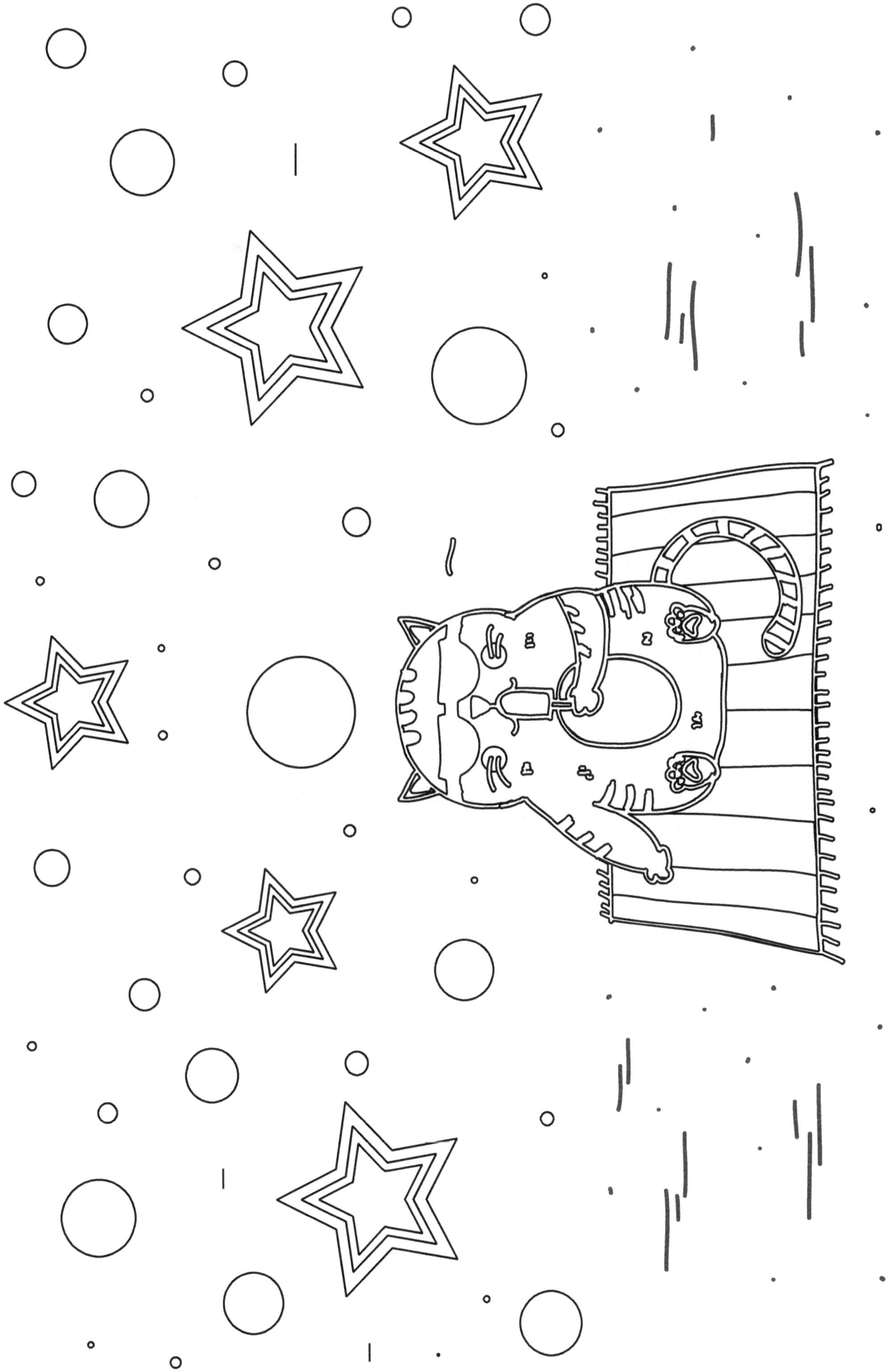

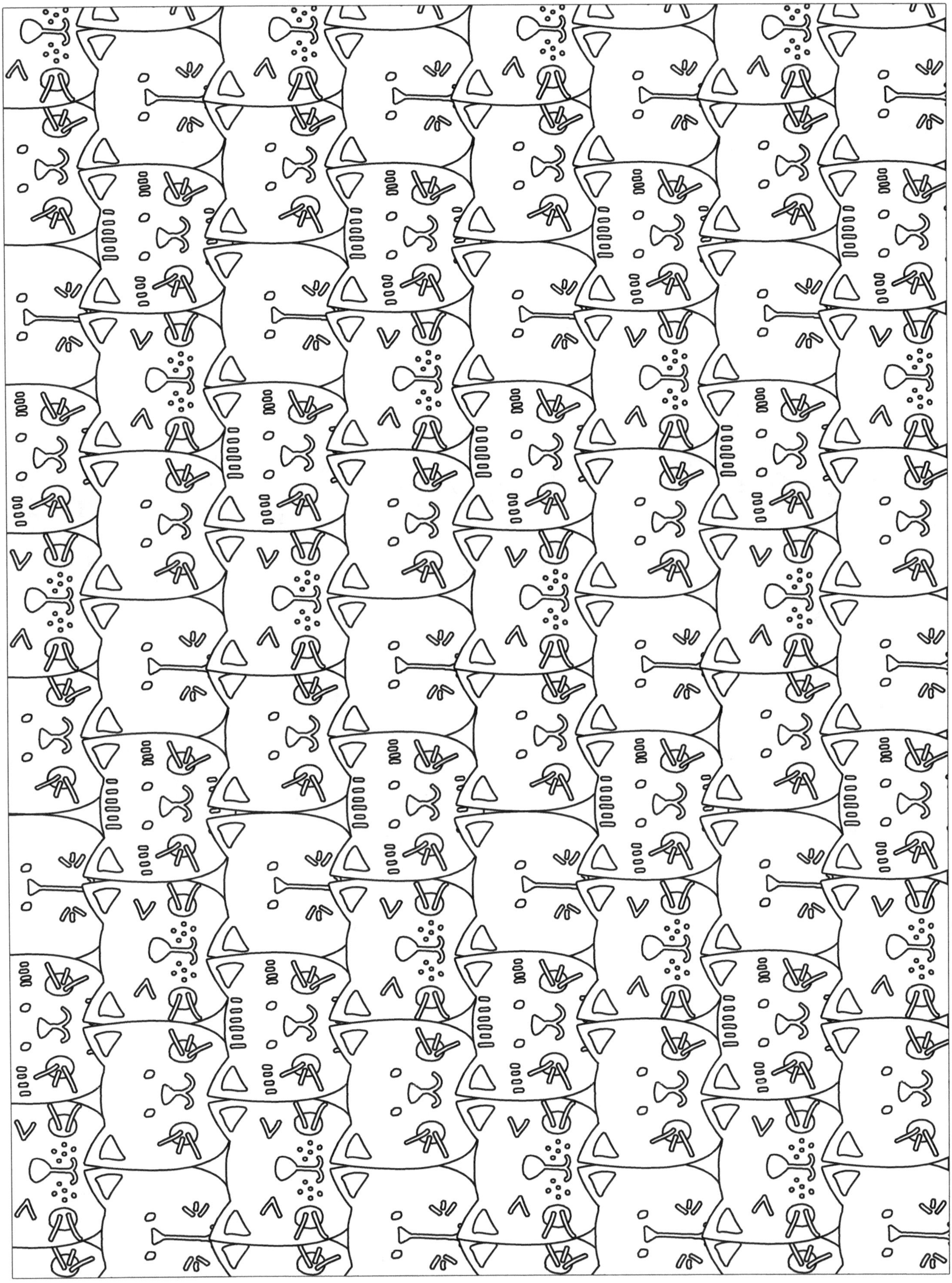

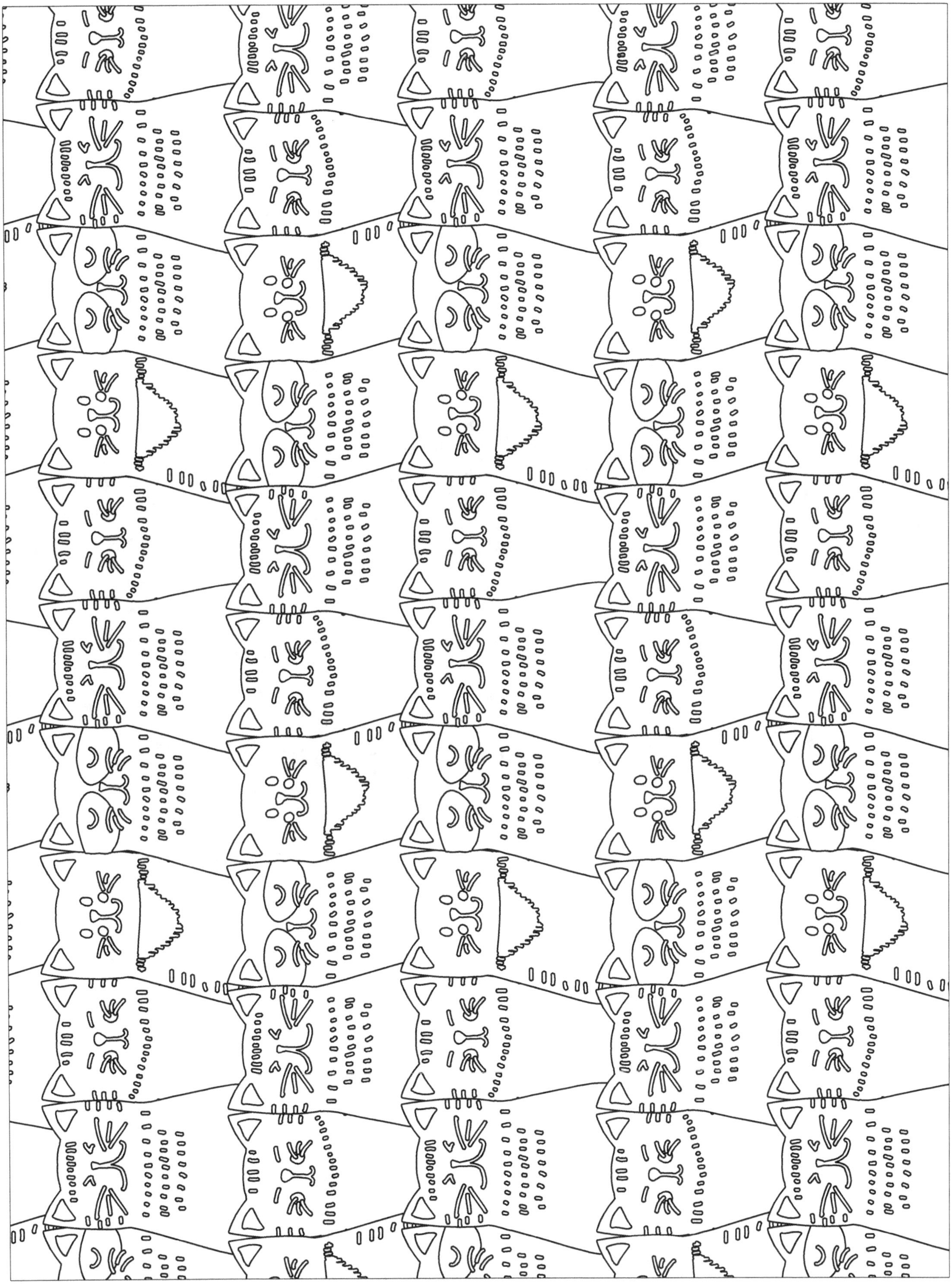

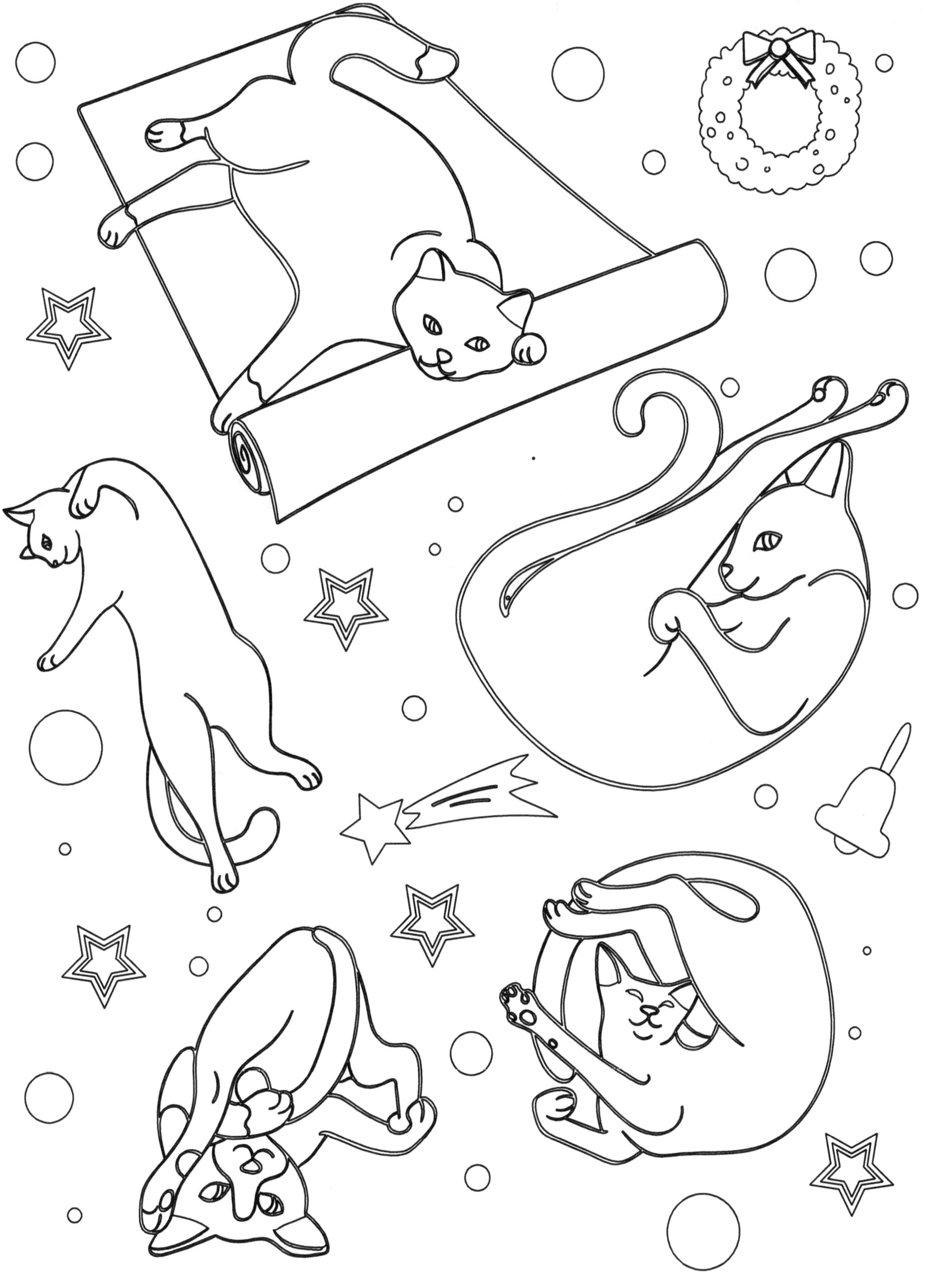

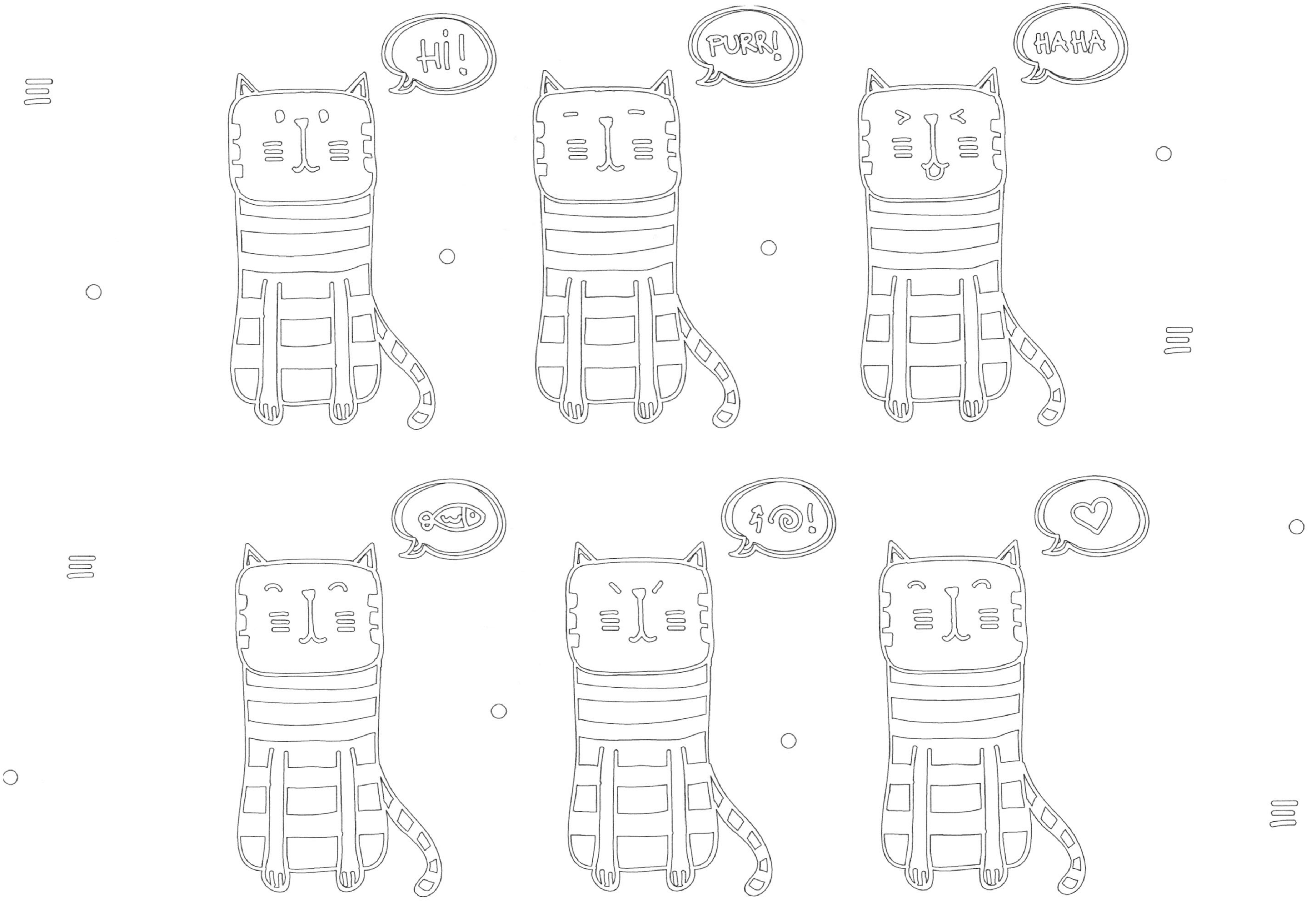
Hi!
PURR!
HAHA

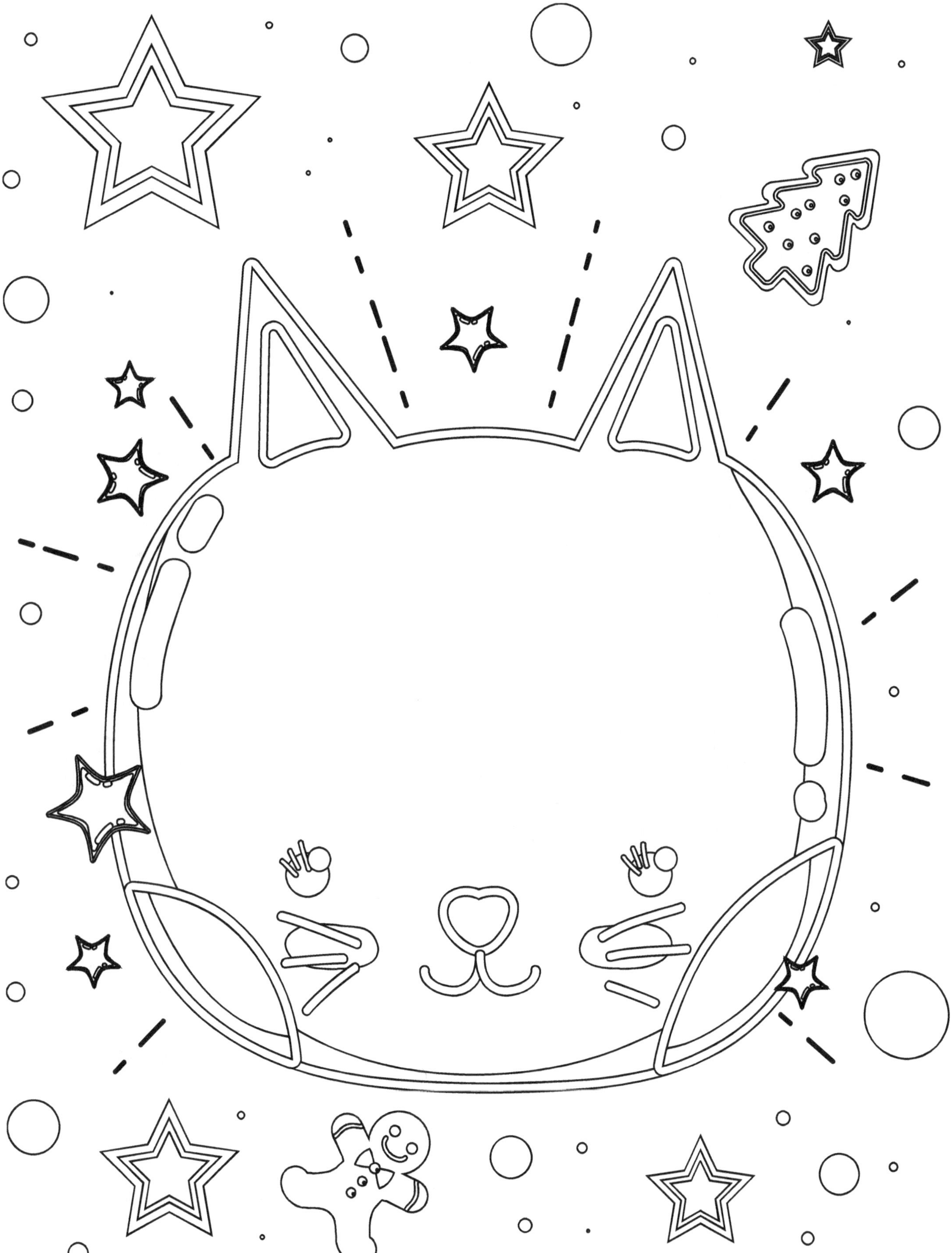

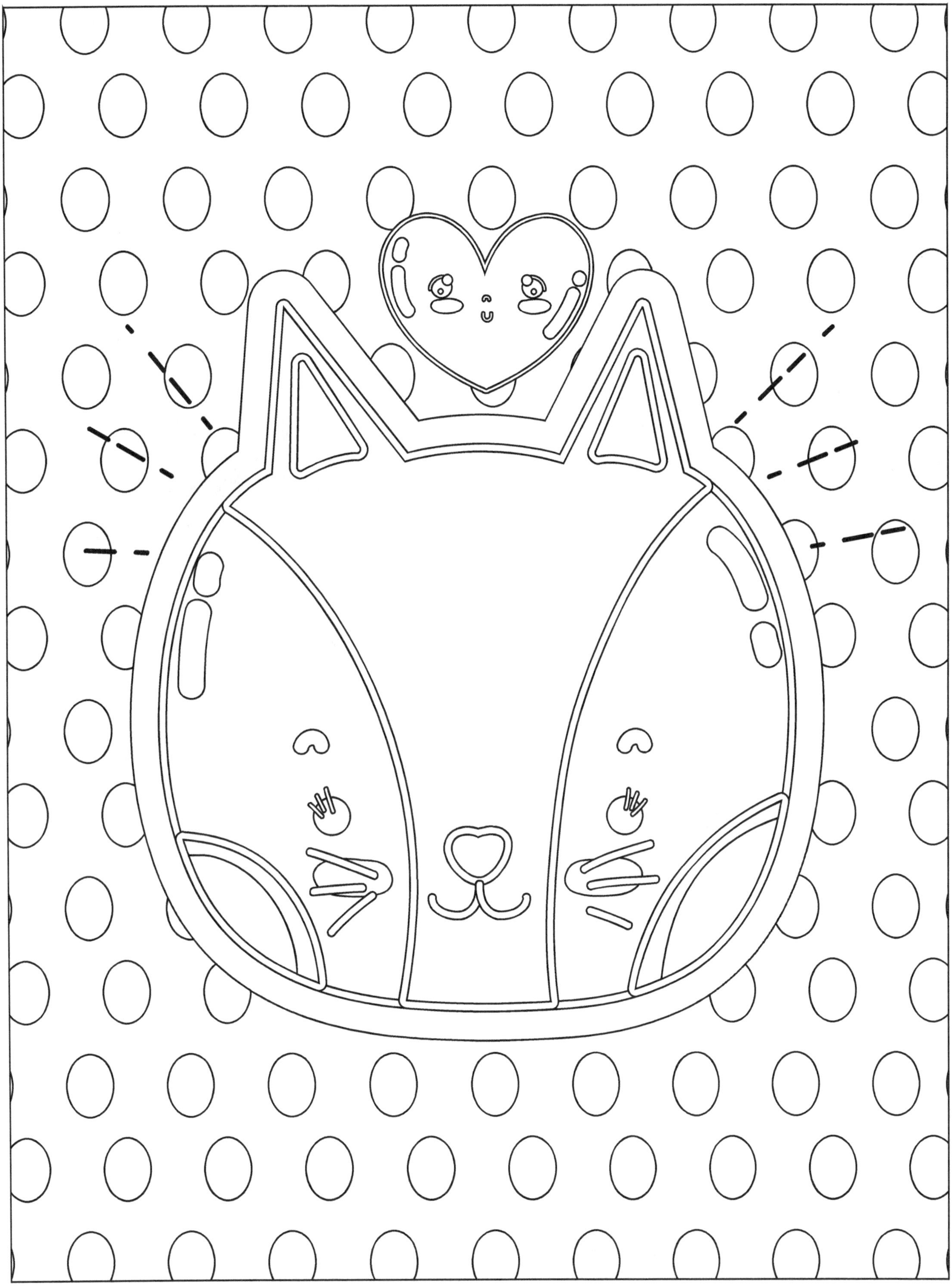

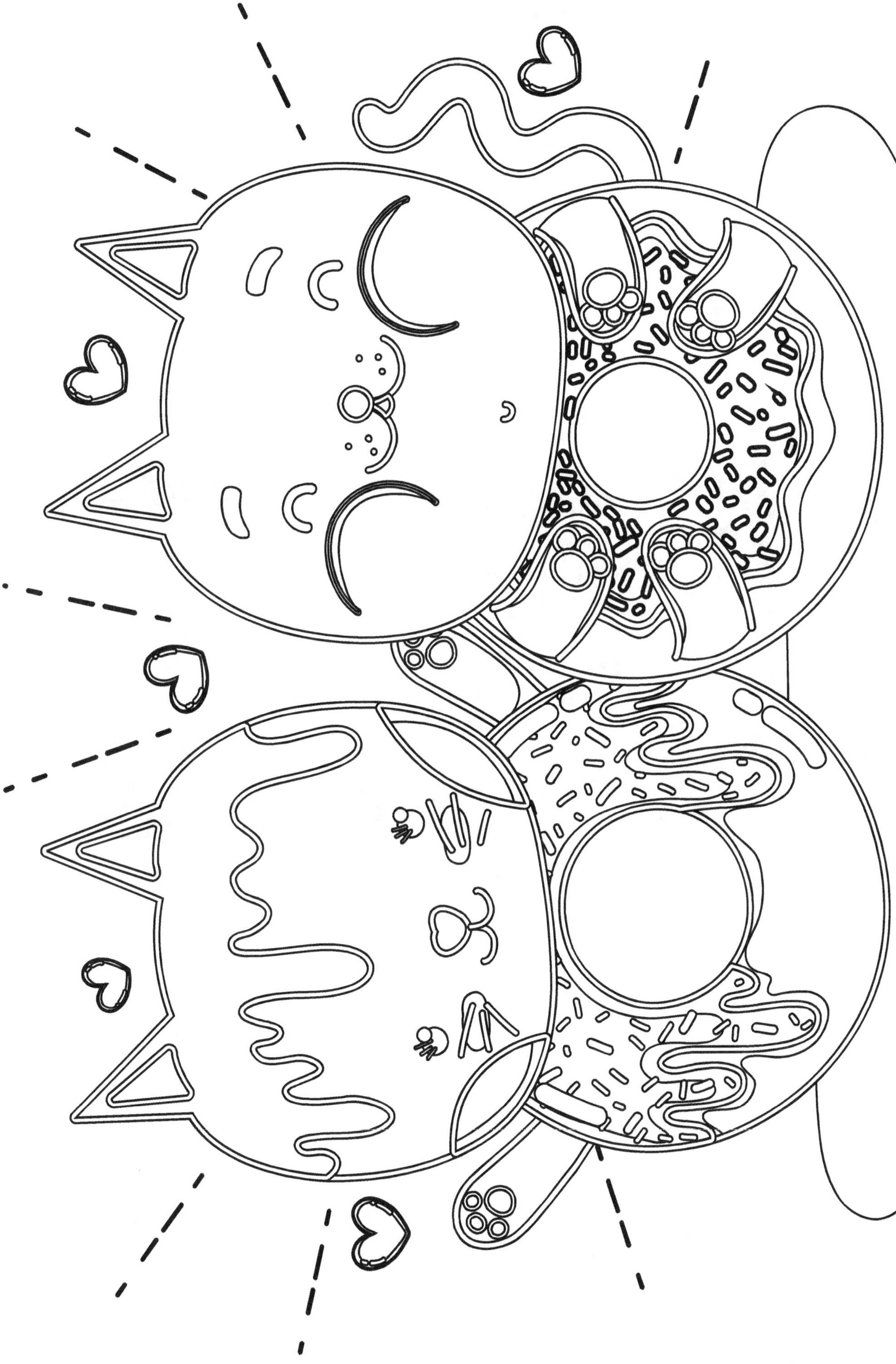

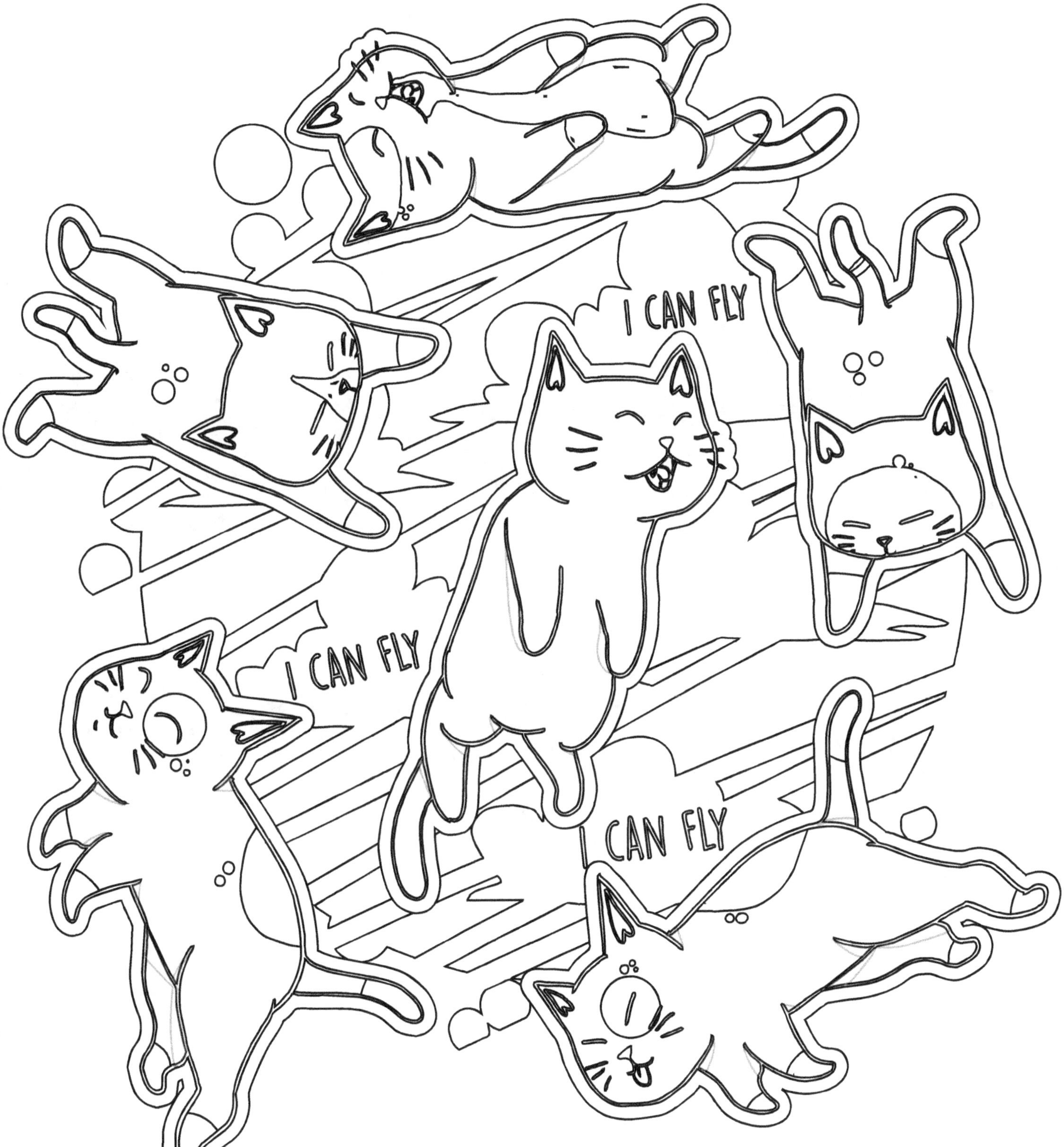
I CAN FLY
I CAN FLY
I CAN FLY

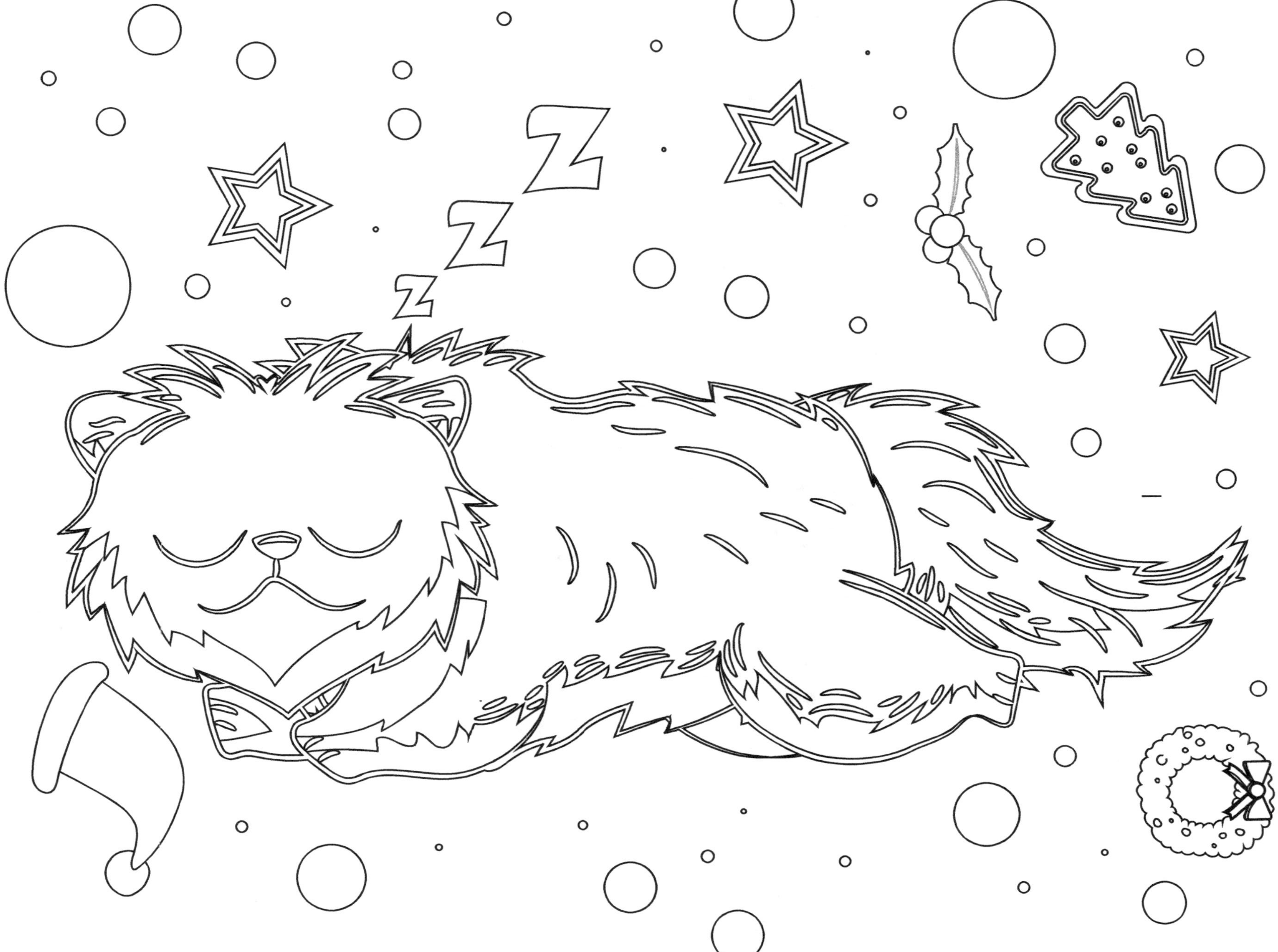
ZZZ

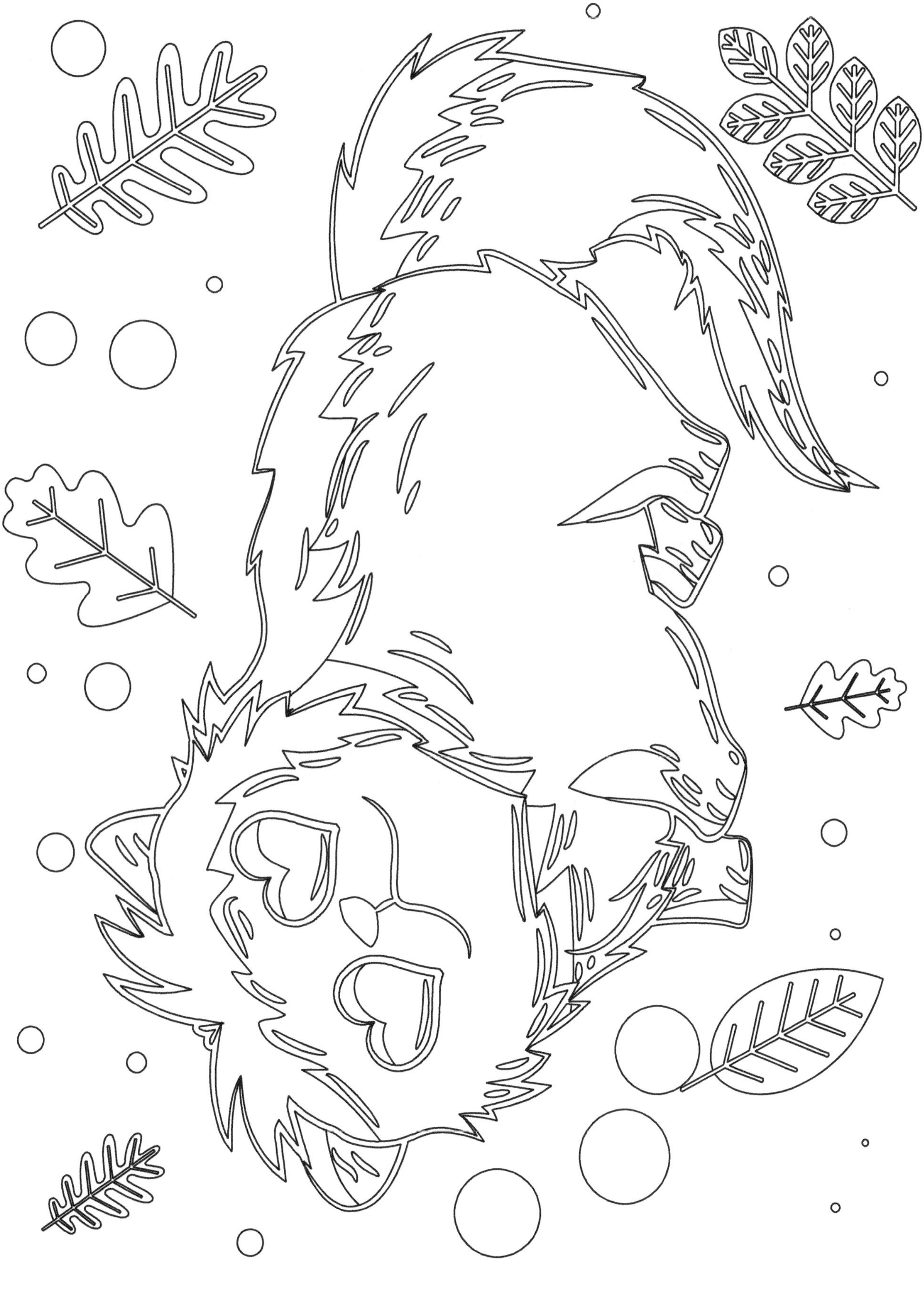

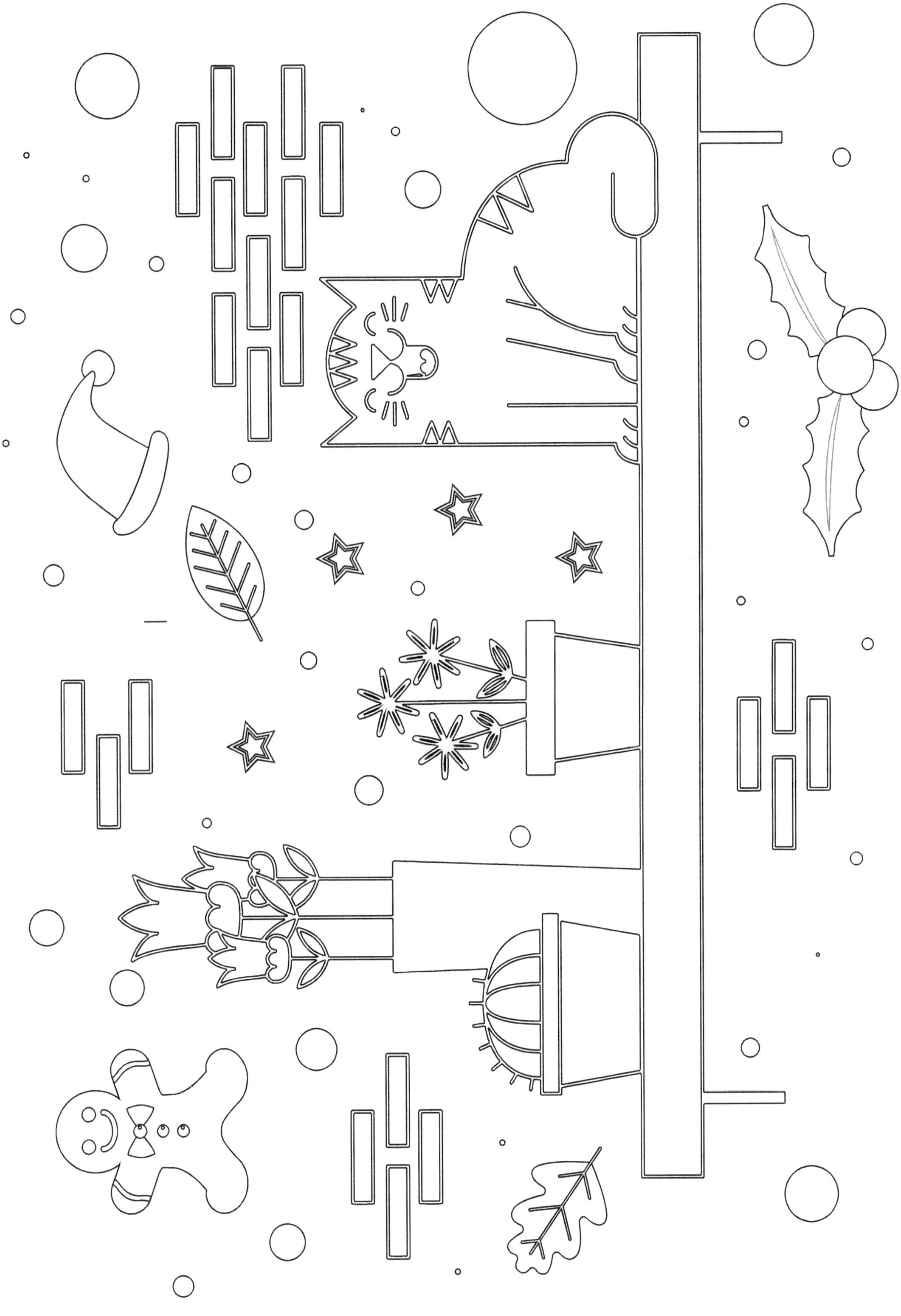

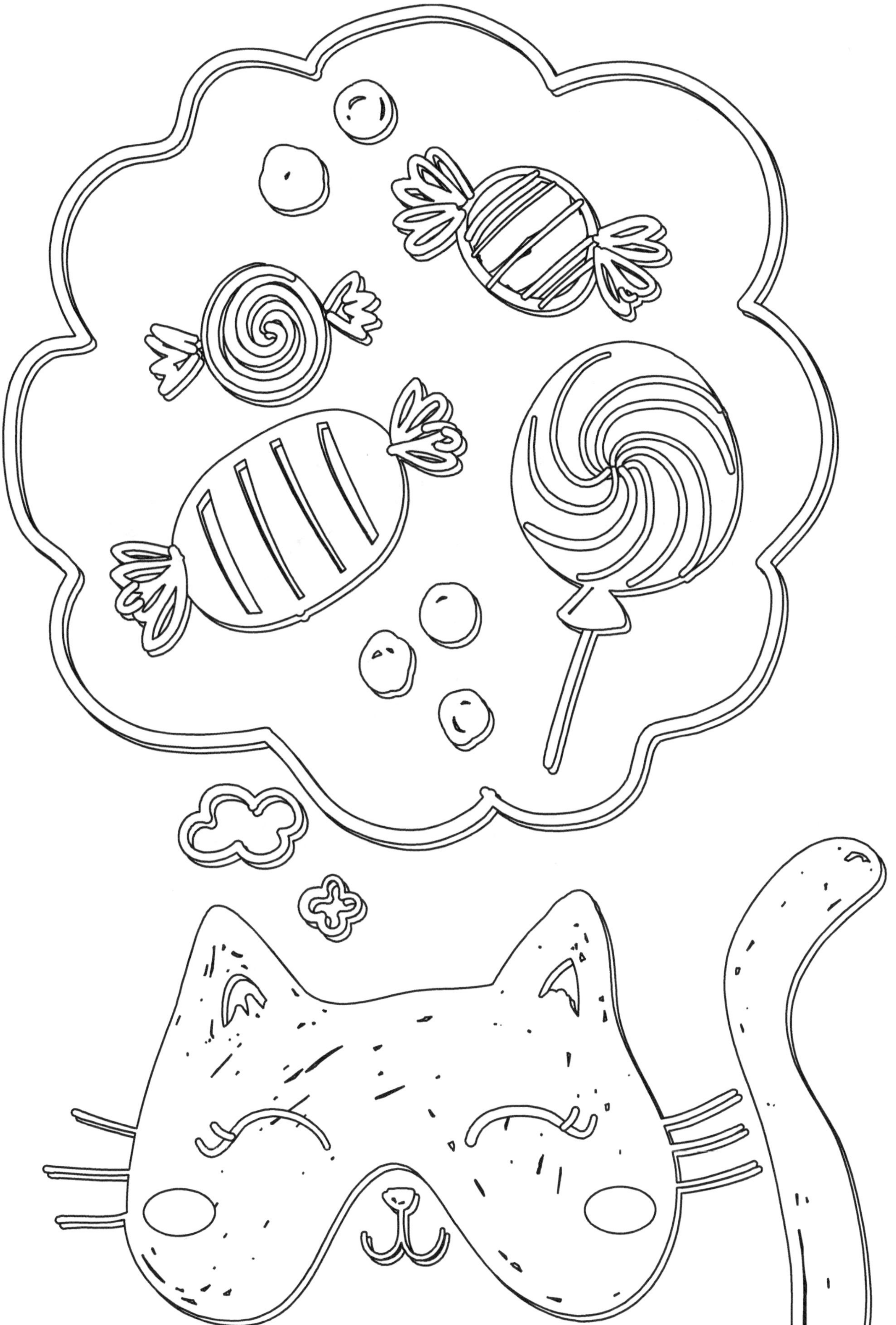

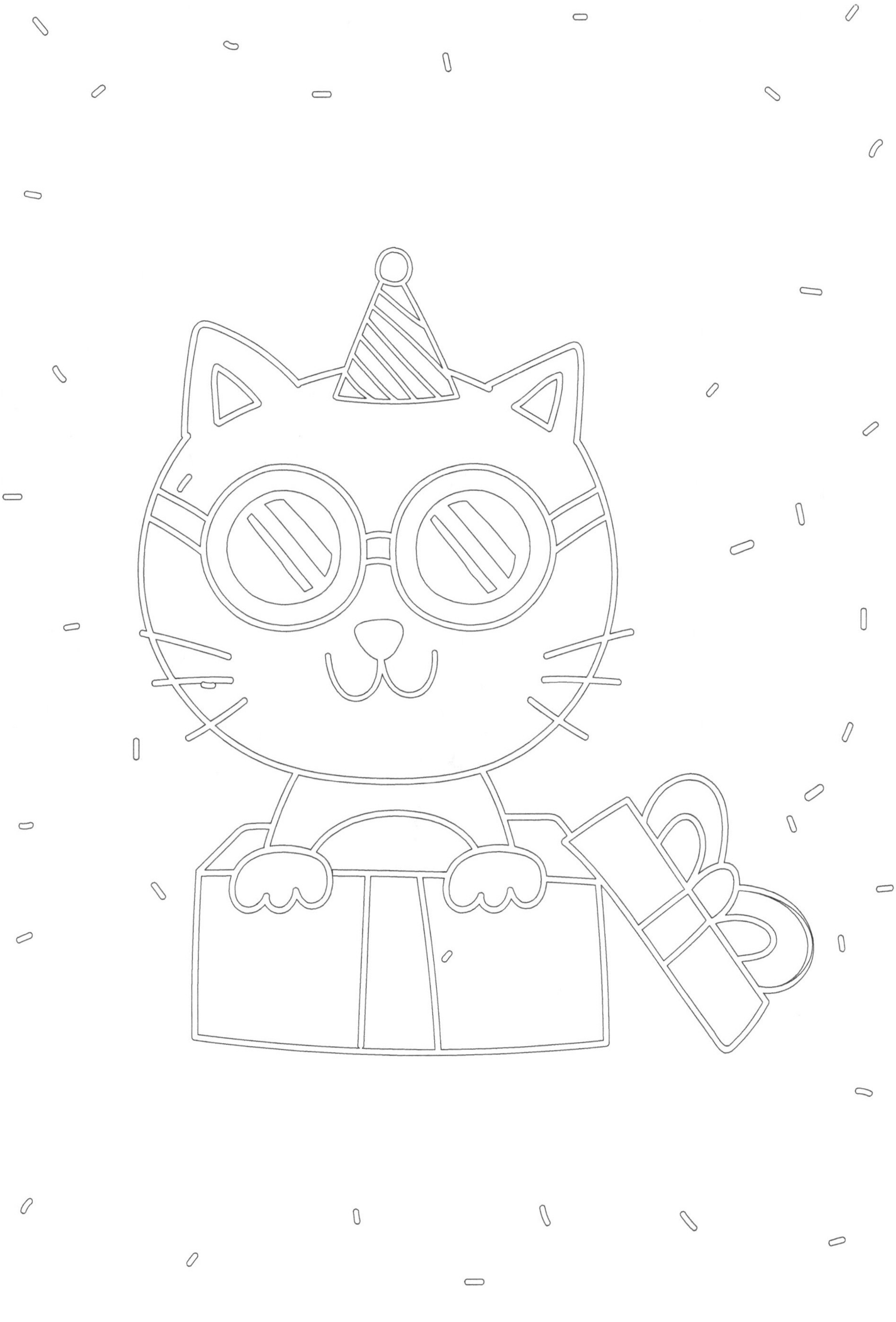

Relax time

www.ingramcontent.com/pod-product-compliance
Lightning Source LLC
Chambersburg PA
CBHW060426220526
45465CB00008B/3031
* 9 7 9 8 6 7 3 3 2 6 9 0 9 *